T0305753

MODELS OF BOUNDED RATIONALITY AND MECHANISM DESIGN

World Scientific Series in Economic Theory
(ISSN: 2251-2071)

Series Editor: Eric Maskin *(Harvard University, USA)*

Published

Forthcoming

World Scientific Series in Economic Theory – Vol. 7

MODELS OF BOUNDED RATIONALITY AND MECHANISM DESIGN

Jacob Glazer

Tel Aviv University, Israel & The University of Warwick, UK

Ariel Rubinstein

Tel Aviv University, Israel & New York University, USA

World Scientific

NEW JERSEY · LONDON · SINGAPORE · BEIJING · SHANGHAI · HONG KONG · TAIPEI · CHENNAI · TOKYO

Published by

World Scientific Publishing Co. Pte. Ltd.

5 Toh Tuck Link, Singapore 596224

USA office: 27 Warren Street, Suite 401-402, Hackensack, NJ 07601

UK office: 57 Shelton Street, Covent Garden, London WC2H 9HE

Library of Congress Cataloging-in-Publication Data
Names: Glazer, Jacob, author. | Rubinstein, Ariel, author.
Title: Models of bounded rationality and mechanism design /
    Jacob Glazer (Tel Aviv University, Israel & The University of Warwick, UK),
    Ariel Rubinstein (Tel Aviv University, Israel & New York University, USA).
Description: New Jersey : World Scientific, [2016] | Series: World Scientific
    series in economic theory ; volume 7 | Includes bibliographical references.
Identifiers: LCCN 2016020984 | ISBN 9789813141322
Subjects: LCSH: Rational expectations (Economic theory) | Game theory. |
    Economics, Mathematical.
Classification: LCC HB3731 .R83 2016 | DDC 330.01/5193--dc23
LC record available at https://lccn.loc.gov/2016020984

British Library Cataloguing-in-Publication Data
A catalogue record for this book is available from the British Library.

Desk Editors: Sandhya Venkatesh/Shreya Gopi

Typeset by Stallion Press
Email: enquiries@stallionpress.com

Printed in Singapore

Contents

Introduction

This book brings together our joint papers from over a period of more than twenty years. The collection includes seven papers, each of which presents a novel and rigorous model in Economic Theory.

All of the models are within the domain of implementation and mechanism design theories. These theories attempt to explain how incentive schemes and organizations can be designed with the goal of inducing agents to behave according to the designer's (principal's) objectives. Most of the literature assumes that agents are fully rational. In contrast, we inject into each model an element which conflicts with the standard notion of full rationality. Following are some examples of such elements: (i) The principal may be constrained in the amount and complexity of the information he can absorb and process. (ii) Agents may be constrained in their ability to understand the rules of the mechanism. (iii) The agent's ability to cheat effectively depends on the complexity involved in finding an effective lie. We will demonstrate how such elements can dramatically change the mechanism design problem.

Although all of the models presented in this volume touch on mechanism design issues, it is the formal modeling of bounded rationality that we are most interested in. By a model of bounded rationality we mean a model that contains a procedural element of reasoning that is not consistent with full rationality. We are not looking for a canonical model of bounded rationality but rather we wish to introduce a variety of modeling devices that will capture procedural elements not previously considered and which alter the analysis of the model.

We suggest that the reader view the book as a journey into the modeling of bounded rationality. It is a collection of modeling ideas rather than a general alternative theory of implementation.

For one of us, this volume is a continuation of work done on modeling bounded rationality since the early eighties (for a partial survey, see Rubinstein (1998)).

A. Implementation with boundedly rational agents

The most representative papers of this collection are the most recent ones ([6] and [7]). Both of them (as well as some of our other papers discussed later on) analyze a situation that we refer to as a persuasion situation.

In a persuasion situation, there is a listener (a principal) and a speaker (an agent). The speaker is characterized by a "profile" (type) that is unknown to the listener but known to the speaker. From the listener's point of view, the set of the listener's possible profiles is divided into two groups: "good" and "bad" and he would like to ascertain to which of the two groups the speaker belongs, in order to decide whether to "accept" him (if he is "good") or to "reject" him (if he is "bad"). The speaker, on the other hand, would like to be accepted regardless of his type. The speaker can send a message to the listener or present some evidence on the basis of which the listener will make a decision. The situation is analyzed as a Stackelberg leader-follower situation, where the listener is the leader (the principal or the planner of a system) who can commit to how he will react to the speaker's moves.

In both papers ([6] and [7]) we build on the idea that the speaker's ability to cheat is limited, a fact that can be exploited by the listener in trying to learn the speaker's type. In [6] each speaker's profile is a vector of zeros and ones. The listener announces a set of rules and commits to accepting every speaker who, when asked to reveal his profile, declares a profile satisfying these rules. A speaker can lie about his profile and had he been fully rational would always come up with a profile that satisfies the set of rules and gets him accepted. We assume, however, that the speaker is boundedly rational and follows a particular procedure in order to find an acceptable profile. The success of this procedure depends on the speaker's true profile. The procedure starts with the speaker checking whether his true profile is acceptable (i.e., whether it satisfies the rules announced by the listener) and if it is, he simply declares it. If the true profile does not satisfy the rules, the speaker attempts to find an acceptable declaration by switching some of the zeros and ones in his true profile in order to make it acceptable. In his attempt to come up with an acceptable profile, the speaker is guided by the rules announced by the listener; any switch of zeros and ones is intended to avoid a violation of one of the rules, even though it might lead to the violation of a different one. The principal knows the procedure that the agent is following and aims to construct the rules in such a way that only the "good" types will be able to come up with an acceptable profile (which may not be their true profile), while the "bad" types who follow the same procedure will fail. In other words, the principal presents the agent with a "puzzle" which, given the particular procedure that the speaker follows, only the speakers with a "good" profile will be able to solve. The paper formalizes the above idea and characterizes the set of profiles that can be implemented, given the procedure that the agents follow.

In [7], we formalize the idea that by cleverly designing a complex questionnaire regarding the speaker's type, the listener can minimize the probability of a dishonest speaker being able to cheat effectively. One important assumption in the paper states that the speaker is ignorant of the listener's objective (namely, which types he would like to accept) but he can obtain some valuable information about the acceptable responses to the questionnaire by observing the set of acceptable responses. We assume that there are both honest and dishonest speakers. Honest speakers simply answer the questionnaire according to their true profile while the dishonest ones try to come up with acceptable answers. The key assumption is that even though a dishonest speaker can observe the set of acceptable responses, he cannot mimic any particular response and all he can do is detect regularities in this set. Given the speaker's limited ability, we show that the listener can design a questionnaire and a set of accepted responses that (i) will treat honest speakers properly, i.e., will accept a response if and only if it is a response of an honest agent of a type that should be accepted) and (ii) will make the probability of a dishonest speaker succeeding arbitrarily small.

B. Mechanisms with a boundedly rational principal

Three of the papers in this collection [3, 4, 5] deal with persuasion situations where the listener is limited in his ability to process the speaker's statements or verify the pieces of evidence provided to him by the speaker.

The most basic paper of the three [5] is chronologically the last one. The following simple example demonstrates the main ideas of the paper: Suppose that the speaker has access to the realization of five independent signals, each of which can receive a value of zero or one (with equal probability). The listener would like to be persuaded if and only if the majority of the signals receive the value 1. Assume that the speaker can provide the listener with hard evidence of the realization of each of the five signals. The speaker cannot lie but he can choose what information to reveal. The key assumption states that the speaker is limited in the amount of information he can provide to the listener and, more specifically, he cannot provide him with the realization of more than (any) two signals. One way to interpret this is that the listener is limited in his (cognitive) ability to verify and fully understand more than two pieces of information. The listener commits in advance as to how he will respond to any evidence presented to him. One can see that if the listener is persuaded by any two supporting pieces of information (i.e. any "state of the world" where two pieces of information support the speaker), the probability of him making the wrong decision is $10/32$. If instead the listener partitions the set of five signals into two sets and commits to being persuaded only by two supporting pieces of evidence coming from the same cell in the partition, then the probability of making a mistake is reduced to its minimal possible level of $4/32$. The paper analyses such persuasion situations in more general terms and characterizes the listener's optimal persuasion rules.

In [3], we study a similar situation, except that instead of one speaker there are two (in this case debaters), each trying to persuade the listener to take his favored action. Each of the two debaters has access to the (same) realization of five signals and, as in the previous case, the listener can understand or verify at most two realizations. The listener commits to a persuasion rule that specifies the order in which the debaters can present hard evidence (the realizations of the signals) and a function that determines, for every two pieces of evidence, which debater he finds persuasive. The listener's objective is to design the persuasion rule in a way that will minimize the probability of him choosing the action supported by two or less signals. It is shown that the lowest probability of choosing the wrong action is $3/32$. The optimal mechanism for the listener consists of first asking one debater to present a realization of one signal that supports his (the first debater's) desired action and then asking the other debater to present a realization of another signal that supports his (the second debater's) preferred action, from a pre-specified set of elements, which depends on the first debater's move. In other words, if we think of the evidence presented by the first debater as an "argument" in his favor, then we can think of the evidence presented by the second debater as a "counterargument". A mechanism defines for every argument, what will be considered a persuasive counterargument.

In [4], the speaker (privately) observes the realization of two random variables, referred to in the paper as "aspects". The speaker can tell the listener what the values of these two random variables are and the listener can verify the value of each but he is cognitively limited to verifying at most one. The listener commits to a rule (not necessarily deterministic) that determines which aspect he will check for every statement the speaker makes and, based on the results, whether or not he will accept the speaker's request. In the main example presented in the paper, the speaker receives information about two independent relevant aspects, each distributed uniformly in the interval $[0, 1]$. The listener wishes to accept the speaker's request if and only if the sum of the realizations of the two aspects is at least 1. We show that the optimal mechanism in this case involves no randomization: the listener simply asks the speaker to declare one aspect and is persuaded if and only if the value of that aspect is found to be above $2/3$. This rule induces a probability of error of $1/6$ on the side of the listener.

In all three papers, we try to interpret the model and its results from the perspective of Pragmatics. Pragmatics is the field of study within Linguistics which investigates the principles that guide us in interpreting an utterance in daily discourse in a way that might be inconsistent with its purely logical meaning. According to our approach, the persuasion rules can be thought of as rules designed by a fictitious designer in order to facilitate communication between individuals. Standard Pragmatics relates mainly to conversation situations, where the involved parties have the common goal of sharing relevant information. We use these models to suggest rationales for pragmatic principles in situations such as persuasion or debate where the interests of the involved parties typically do not coincide.

C. The choice of equilibrium concept in implementation problems

The first paper [1] marks the beginning of our collaboration. It is related to a long-standing discussion in the implementation literature of the appropriate solution concept to be applied to games induced by a mechanism. The paper contributed to this discussion by comparing the sophistication required of agents when applying two different solution concepts: subgame perfect equilibrium and iterative elimination of dominated strategies.

More precisely, consider a mechanism designer who designs a solvable normal form game such that for each profile of agents' preferences the outcome that survives successive elimination of dominated strategies is exactly the one the designer would like to implement. Calculating the strategy that survives iterative elimination of dominated strategies in the designed normal form game may be not trivial for agents. Implementation would be easier if the designer could supply each agent with a "guide" that instructs him how to conduct the iterative elimination process. We argue that the design of a normal form game with such a guide is equivalent to the design of an extensive game solved by backward induction. In other words, the extensive game serves as a guide for the agents in deciding which strategy to play.

D. Implementation with behavioral motives

The last paper in the volume [2] is, to the best of our knowledge, one of the first papers in theoretical behavioral economics. As such, it is a somewhat of an outlier in this collection which deals mainly with models of bounded rationality. The context of the paper is a standard "committee" model in which there are several experts, each of whom receives an independent informative signal (0 or 1) indicating which action is the correct one. The principal's objective is to design a mechanism such that regardless of the profile of the experts' views, the only equilibrium of the mechanism game is such that the principal chooses the action supported by the majority of the signals. Our first observation is that if each expert cares only about increasing the probability that the right decision is made, no mechanism will eliminate equilibria in which the signal observed by only one expert determines the outcome. However, the situation changes if a particular behavioral element is introduced: Assume that if during the play of the mechanism an expert is asked to make a recommendation regarding which action should be chosen, then, in addition to sharing the common goal that the right action (i.e., the one supported by the signals observed by the majority of the experts) be chosen, the expert also cares that his recommendation will coincide with the one that is eventually chosen. We show that, surprisingly, if each expert is driven by a combination of the public motive (that the right action be chosen) and the private motive (that his recommendation be accepted), the designer can construct a mechanism such that there will always be a unique equilibrium outcome where all experts report their signal truthfully and the action supported by the majority of the signals is adopted.

As mentioned above, this book is primarily a presentation of innovative ways to model bounded rationality in economic settings. Some of the issues in modeling bounded rationality in economics were previously discussed and surveyed in Rubinstein (1998) and Spiegler (2011).

The book is also part of the literature on mechanism design, and thus we feel obliged to mention some papers that are directly related to implementation with bounded rationality and which were, in our opinion, among the first to include elements of bounded rationality within implementation theory.

Hurwicz (1986) studies implementation theory in a world where the agents are teams with patterns of behavior that cannot be captured by just maximizing preferences.

Eliaz (2002) is a pioneering attempt to determine which social choice functions can be implemented when players know each other's private information, but some "faulty" players may behave in an unpredictable manner.

Crawford, Kugler, Neeman and Pauzner (2009) were the first to investigate implementation when the standard equilibrium concept is replaced with "k-level rationality".

De Clippel (2014) is an impressive study of the classical implementation problem where players are described by choice functions that satisfy certain properties but are not necessarily rationalizable (see also Korpela (2012), Ray (2010) and Saran (2011)).

Cabrales and Serrano (2011) investigate implementation problems under the behavioral assumption that agents myopically adjust their actions in the direction of better responses or best responses.

Jehiel (2011) employs the analogy-based expectation equilibrium in the context of designing an auction problem.

An early work related to our approach of studying persuasion situations is Green and Laffont (1986) who analyze a revelation mechanism where the agent is restricted as to the messages he can submit to the principal.

Chapter 1

An Extensive Game as a Guide for Solving a Normal Game*

Jacob Glazer

Faculty of Management, Tel Aviv University

Ariel Rubinstein

School of Economics, Tel-Aviv University, and
Department of Economics, Princeton University

We show that for solvable games, the calculation of the strategies which survive iterative elimination of dominated strategies in normal games is equivalent to the calculation of the backward induction outcome of some extensive game. However, whereas the normal game form does not provide information on how to carry out the elimination, the corresponding extensive game does. As a by-product, we conclude that implementation using a subgame perfect equilibrium of an extensive game with perfect information is equivalent to implementation through a solution concept which we call guided iteratively elimination of dominated strategies which requires a uniform order of elimination.

Journal of Economic Literature Classification Numbers: C72.

1. Introduction

Game theory usually interprets a game form as a representation of the physical rules which govern a strategic interaction. However, one can view a game form more abstractly as a description of a systematic relationship between players' preferences and the outcome of the situation. Consider, for example, a situation which involves two players, 1 and 2. The players can go

*The first author acknowledges financial support from the Israel Institute of Business Research. The second author acknowledges partial financial support from the United States–Israel Binational Science Foundation, Grant Number 1011-341. We thank Paolo Battigiali, an associate editor, and a referee of this Journal, for their excellent comments on the first version of this paper.

1

out to either of two places of entertainment, T or B, bringing with them a third (passive) party L or R. The two players have preferences over the four possible combinations of place and companion. The three presuppositions regarding the situation are:

(i) Player 2's preferences over the companion component are independent of the place of entertainment.
(ii) Player 2 decides on L or R.
(iii) Player 1 decides on T or B.

Game theory suggests two models to describe this situation. One model would describe the players as playing the game G (see Fig. 1) with the outcome determined by the solution of successive elimination of weakly dominated strategies. The other would say that the players are involved in the game Γ (see Fig. 2) and that the solution concept is one of backward

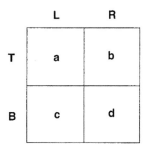

Figure 1.

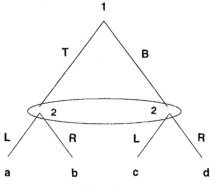

Figure 2.

induction. Each alternative summarizes all of the information we possess about the situation. However, the description of the situation via an extensive game is more informative than that via a normal game form since the former provides a guide for easier calculation of the outcome for any given profile of preferences which is consistent with (i).

In this paper we elaborate on this idea. We begin in Section 2 by introducing the notion of a "guide" for solving normal form games through iterative elimination of dominated strategies. A guide is a sequence of instructions regarding the order of elimination. In Section 3 we establish that the information about the procedure of solving a normal form game provided by the guide is essentially identical to the additional information provided when the game is described in its extensive form rather than its normal form. As a by-product, we show in Section 4 that implementation by subgame perfect equilibrium (SPE) in an extensive game is equivalent to implementation through a solution concept, which we call guided iteratively undominated strategies, in a normal game which requires a uniform order of elimination.

2. Preliminaries

Let N be a set of players and C a set of consequences. A preference profile is a vector of preferences over C, one preference for each player. In order to simplify the paper we confine our analysis to preferences which exclude indifferences between consequences.

(a) *Normal Game Form*

A *normal game form* is $G = \langle \times_{i \in N} S_i, g \rangle$, where S_i is i's strategy space and $g \colon \times_{i \in N} S_i \to C$ is the consequence function. (Without any loss of generality, assume that no strategy in S_i has the name of a subset of S_i.) A game form G accompanied by a preference profile $p = \{\geq_i\}_{i \in N}$ is a *normal game* denoted by $\langle G, p \rangle$. We say that the strategy $s_i \in S_i$ *dominates* the strategy $s_i' \in S_i$ if $g(s_i, s_{-i}) \geq_i g(s_i', s_{-i})$ for any profile $s_{-i} \in \times_{j \neq i} S_j$. By this definition one strategy dominates the other even if $g(s_i, s_{-i}) = g(s_i', s_{-i})$ for all s_{-i}.

(b) *Guide*

A guide for a normal form G is a list of instructions for solving games of the type $\langle G, p \rangle$. Each instruction k consists of a name of player i_k and a set A_k. The sublist of instructions for which $i_k = i$ can be thought of as a "multi-round tournament" whose participants are the strategies in S_i. The first instruction in this sublist is a set of at least 2 strategies for player i. One of these strategies will be thought of as a winner (in a sense that will be described later). The losers leave the tournament and the winner receives the name of the subset in which he won. Any element in the sublist is a subset of elements which are left in the tournament. Such an element is either a strategy in S_i which has not participated in any previous round of the tournament, or a strategy which won all previous rounds in which it participated; this strategy appears under the name of the last round in which it won. Following completion of the last round, only one strategy of player i remains a non-loser. Thus, for example, if $S_1 = \{x_1, x_2, x_3, x_4, x_5\}$, a possible sublist for player 1 is $A_1 = \{x_1, x_2\}$, $A_2 = \{x_3, x_4\}$, and $A_3 = \{A_1, A_2, x_5\}$. In the first round, x_1 and x_2 are "compared." In the second round, the strategies x_3 and x_4 are compared and in the final round x_5 and the winners of the previous two rounds are compared. The guide is an order in which the strategies are compared, but it does not contain the rules by which one strategy is declared a winner in any particular round.

Formally, a (finite) *guide* for G is a sequence $(i_k, A_k)_{k=1,\dots,K}$ satisfying:

(i) For every k, $i_k \in N$.

(ii) For every k' with $i_{k'} = i$, $A_{k'}$ is a set with at least two elements where each element in the set is either a strategy in S_i or a set A_k with $i_k = i$ and $k < k'$.

(iii) Let k_i^* be the largest k with $i_k = i$. Each strategy in S_i and each set A_k with $i_k = i$ and $k < k_i^*$ is a member of a single set $A_{k'}$ with $i_{k'} = i$.

So far we have only defined the structure of the tournament and have yet to describe how a winner is selected in each round. A winner in round k is an element of A_k which dominates the other elements according to player i_k's preferences in the game in which all the losers in the previous $k - 1$ rounds were eliminated. A guide for G solves a game $\langle G, p \rangle$ if, when applying the guide, there is a winner in each round. Our formal definition is inductive: The guide $D = (i_k, A_k)_{k=1,\dots,K}$ *solves the game* $G = \langle \times_{i \in N} S_i, g, p \rangle$ if

(i) there is an $a^* \in A_1$ which dominates all strategies in A_1 and

(ii) for $K > 1$, the guide $D' = (i_{k+1}, A_{k+1})_{k=1,\dots,K-1}$ solves the game G' which is obtained from G by omitting all of i_1's strategies in A_1 and adding one new strategy called A_1 to player i_1's set of strategies so that $g'(A_1, a_{-i_1}) = g(a^*, a_{-i_1})$.

Thus, for the guide to solve the game it must be that in every stage there is a dominating strategy. Note that by the assumption of no-indifference, if there are two dominating strategies a^* and b^* then $g(a^*, a_{-i_1}) = g(b^*, a_{-i_1})$ for all a_{-i_1} and thus the definition of G' does not depend on which of these strategies is declared a winner.

Note that by condition (iii) in the definition of a guide, if D solves the game $\langle G, p \rangle$, then the game which is obtained in the last stage has one strategy for each player. The consequence attached to the surviving profile of strategies is called the *D-guided I-outcome*.

The notion of iterative elimination of dominated strategies can be stated, using our guide terminology, as follows: a consequence z survives the iterative elimination of dominated strategies and, in short, is an I-outcome of the game $\langle G, p \rangle$, if there is some guide D, such that z is a D-guided I-outcome of $\langle G, p \rangle$.

(c) *Extensive Game Form*

A (finite) *extensive game form* is a four-tuple $\Gamma = \langle H, i, I, g \rangle$, where:

(i) H is a finite set of sequences called histories (nodes) such that the empty sequence is in H and if $(a_1, \ldots, a_t) \in H$ then $(a_1, \ldots, a_{t-1}) \in H$.

(ii) i is a function which assigns to any non-terminal history $h \in H$ a name of a player who has to move at the history h (a history $(a_1, \ldots, a_t)$ is non-terminal if there is an x so that $(a_1, \ldots, a_t, x) \in H$). The set of actions which $i(h)$ has to choose from is $A(h) = \{a | (h, a) \in H\}$.

(iii) I is a partition of the set of non-terminal histories in H such that if h and h' are in the same information set (an element of this partition) then both $i(h) = i(h')$ and $A(h) = A(h')$.

(iv) g is a function which assigns a consequence in C to every terminal history in H.

We confine ourselves to games with perfect recall. A *terminal information set* X is an information set such that for all $h \in X$ and $a \in A(h)$, the history (h, a) is terminal.

The following definition of a game solvable by backward induction is provided for completeness. Simultaneously we will define the B-outcome to be the consequence which is obtained from executing the procedure. Note that our definition rests on weak dominance at information sets.

Let $\Gamma = \langle H, i, I, g \rangle$ be an extensive game form. The game $\langle \Gamma, p \rangle$ is solvable by backward induction if either:

(i) the set of histories in Γ consists of only one history (in this case it can be said that the attached consequence is the B-outcome of the game) or

(ii) Γ includes at least one terminal information set and

    (a) for any terminal information set X and any $h \in X$ there is an action $a^* \subset A(h)$ such that for any $a' \subset A(h)$ we have $y(h, a^*) \succeq_{i(h)} g(h, a')$,

    (b) the game $\langle \Gamma', p \rangle$ is solvable by backward induction where Γ' is obtained from Γ by deleting the histories which follow X and assigning the consequence $g(h, a^*)$ to any $h \in X$.

(Formally, $H' = H - \{(h, a) | h \in X$ and $a \in A(X)\}$, $i'(h) = i(h)$ for any $h \in H'$, $I' = I - \{X\}$ and $g'(h) = g(h, a^*)$ for any $h \in X$ and $g'(h) = g(h)$ for any other terminal history.) The B-outcome of $\langle \Gamma, p \rangle$ is the B-outcome of the game $\langle \Gamma', p \rangle$.

Note that the game form Γ in the above definition can include information sets which are not singletons. It is required that for any such information set there is an action for the player who moves at this point which is better than any other action available at this information set regardless of which history led to it. Therefore, if a game $\langle \Gamma, p \rangle$ is solvable by backward induction then the B-outcome is the unique subgame perfect equilibrium outcome of the game with perfect information which is derived from $\langle \Gamma, p \rangle$ by splitting all information sets into singletons.

(d) *A Normal Form of an Extensive Game Form*

Let Γ be an extensive game form. A *plan of action* for player i is any function s_i which has the property that it assigns a unique action only to those information sets that can be reached by s_i (the information set X is reached if there is at least one $h = (a_1, \ldots, a_T) \in X$ so that for every subhistory $h' = (a_1, \ldots, a_t)$ with $i(h') = i$, $s_i(h') = a_{t+1}$). The notion of a plan of action differs from the notion of a strategy in an extensive game in that it is not defined for information sets that can never be reached given the strategy. Define the *reduced normal form* of Γ to be the normal game form $G(\Gamma) = \langle \times_{i \in N} S_i, g \rangle$, where S_i is the set of all player i's plans of action and $g((s_i)_{i \in N})$ is the consequence reached in Γ if every player i adopts the plan of action s_i.

3. On the Equivalence between a Normal Game Form with a Guide and an Extensive Game Form

In the previous section we distinguished between an I-outcome and a D-guided I-outcome. By stating that z is an I-outcome, no information is given as to the order of elimination, which leads to the observation that z is an I-outcome. On the other hand by stating that z is a D-guided I-outcome not only do we reveal that it is an I-outcome but also that it is an outcome of elimination carried out in the order described by the particular guide D. In this section we argue that an extensive game can be viewed as equivalent to a guide and thus conclude that calculating the subgame perfect equilibrium outcome in an extensive game is simpler than calculating the outcome of an iterative elimination of dominated strategies in a normal game.

The main result of the paper is the following.

Proposition 1. *For every normal game form G and a guide D there is an extensive game form Γ (independent of any preference profile) such that the normal game form of Γ is G and for all p:*

(a) *The guide D solves the normal game $\langle G, p \rangle$ iff the extensive game $\langle \Gamma, p \rangle$ is solvable by backward induction.*

(b) *A consequence z is a D-guided I-outcome of $\langle G, p \rangle$ iff it is a B-outcome of $\langle \Gamma, p \rangle$.*

Furthermore, there is a game with perfect information Γ^* so that for all p, the B-outcome of $\langle \Gamma, p \rangle$ is the same as the subgame perfect equilibrium outcome of $\langle \Gamma^*, p \rangle$.

Proof. Let $G = \langle \times_{i \in N} S_i, g \rangle$ be a game form and $D = (i_k, A_k)_{k=1,\dots,K}$ be a guide. We construct the extensive game form so that the calculations of the I-outcome using the guide from the beginning to the end are equivalent to the calculations of the B-outcome in the extensive game starting from the end and going backward. The construction is done inductively starting from the initial history and using the information contained in the last element of the guide.

As an initial step, assign the history ϕ to i_K. Let the set $\{\phi\}$ be an information set and let $A(\phi) = A_K$. Add to the set of histories all sequences (x) of length one where $x \in A_K$.

Now assume that we have already completed t stages of the construction. For stage $t+1$ look at $k = K - t$. If it is not the largest k' so that $i_{k'} = i_k$ (that is, it is not the first time in the construction that we assign a decision to player i_k), then group into the same information set all terminal histories in the game we have constructed up to the end of stage t in which A_k was chosen. If it is the largest k' so that $i_{k'} = i_k$, then group into the same information set all terminal histories in the game we have constructed up to the end of stage t. Add to the set of histories all histories (h, x) where $x \in A_k$.

When the construction of the set of histories is complete, any terminal history h is a sequence such that for every player i there is a nested subsequence of acts which must end with a choice of a strategy, $s_i(h) \in S_i$. We attach to the terminal history h the consequence attached to $s_i(h)$ in G. It is easy to verify that Γ is a game form with perfect recall. Figure 3 illustrates the construction.

To verify that the normal form of Γ is G, note that any strategy of player i in Γ can be thought of as a choice of one strategy in S_i with the understanding that whenever he has to move he chooses an action which is a set including s_i. Furthermore, the consequence of the terminal history which results from the profile of the extensive game strategies which correspond to $(s_i)_{i \in N}$ was chosen as $g(s)$.

The proof of (a) and (b) follows from two observations:

(i) The first stage of calculating the backward induction in Γ and the first stage in applying D involve precisely the same comparisons. When applying D we look for a strategy $x \in A_1$ which dominates the other members of A_1; such a strategy satisfies that $g(x, a_{-i_1}) \geq_{i_1} g(x', a_{-i_1})$ for all $x' \in A_1$ and for all profiles a_{-i_1}. This is the calculation which is done in the first stage of the backward induction calculation in Γ. The player in the only terminal decision information set is i_1 and he has to choose an action from A_1. Since the game involves perfect recall, along each history in his information set the other players choose a single element in their strategy space. For x to be chosen, it must be that $g(x, h) \geq_{i_1} g(x', h)$ for all h, that is, $g(x, a_{-i_1}) \geq_{i_1} g(x', a_{-i_1})$ for all $x' \in A_1$.

(ii) Denote by $\Gamma(G, D)$ the extensive game form constructed from the normal game form G and the guide D. For every profile p, $\Gamma(G', D') = \Gamma'$, where G' is the normal game form obtained following the execution of the first step of the guide D, D' is the guide starting with the second instruction of D, and Γ' is the extensive game obtained by executing the first step of the backward induction procedure on Γ.

The game G

	r	s	t
a	O_1	O_2	O_3
b	O_4	O_5	O_6
c	O_7	O_8	O_9

The guide D

$i_1 = 1$ $A_1 = \{a, b\}$

$i_2 = 2$ $A_2 = \{r, s\}$

$i_3 = 1$ $A_3 = \{A_1, c\}$

$i_4 = 2$ $A_4 = \{A_2, t\}$

The extensive game

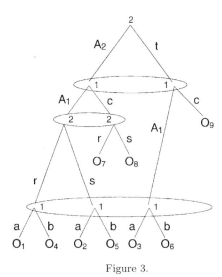

Figure 3.

From the fact that any B-outcome of an extensive game Γ is the subgame perfect equilibrium of the extensive game Γ^* in which all information sets are singletons we conclude that there is a game form with perfect information Γ^* such that for all p, the B-outcome of $\langle \Gamma, p \rangle$ is the same as the subgame perfect equilibrium outcome of $\langle \Gamma^*, p \rangle$.

4. Implementation

It is often felt that implementation theory ignores "complexity" considerations (see Jackson [4]). A proof that a particular class of social functions is implementable frequently utilizes a game form which is messy to describe and complicated to play. It is natural to evaluate implementation devices according to their complexity in order to identify more plausible mechanisms. One component of complexity is the difficulty in calculating the outcome of the mechanism. If the calculation of the I-outcome of a normal form game involves the same comparisons as the backward induction for an extensive game, then the latter may be considered simpler in the sense that it provides the players with a guide for executing the calculation.

Let P be a set of preference profiles over C. A *social function* assigns to every profile $p \in P$ an element in C. We say that a social function f is *I-implementable* by the game form G if for all p, the I-outcome of the game (G, p) is $f(p)$. We say that a social function f is *guided-I-implementable* by the game form G and the guide D if for all p, the D guided I-outcome of the game (G, p) is $f(p)$. In other words, the game G guided-I-implements f if there is *one* guide which solves $\langle G, p \rangle$ for all $p \in P$ and the outcome is $f(p)$. Finally, we say that f is *SPE-implementable* if there is an extensive game form with perfect information Γ so that for all p the subgame perfect equilibrium outcome of the game (Γ, p) is $f(p)$. (Actually this definition is more restrictive than the one of say Moore and Rappulo [5], since only games of perfect information are admitted. It is closer to the definition of Herrero and Strivatsava [3].)

One might conjecture that SPE-implementation is equivalent to I-implementation. This is not the case as demonstrated by the following example (suggested by the first author and Motty Perry).

Example. Let $C = \{a, b, c, d\}$ and let $P = \{\alpha, \beta\}$ where $\alpha = (d >_1 b >_1 c >_1 a, b >_2 c >_2 d >_2 a)$ and $\beta = (b >_1 c >_1 d >_1 a, d >_2 c >_2 b >_2 a)$.

Consider the social function f: $f(\alpha) = c$ and $f(\beta) = b$. The function f is I-implementable by the normal form of the game in Fig. 1: In α, for player 1, B dominates T and, for player 2, L dominates R and the final outcome is c. In β, for player 2, R dominates L and, for player 1, T dominates B and the final outcome is b.

Notice that different orders of elimination were used in the calculation of the two profiles. In α, the elimination starts with the deletion of one of player 1's actions and in β it starts with the deletion of one of player 2's actions.

Although f is I-implementable we will now see that there is no extensive game with perfect information which SPE-implements f. If Γ is an extensive game form which SPE-implements f, then f is also SPE-implemented by a game form Γ' which is derived from Γ by the omission of all terminal histories with the consequence a (since it is the worst consequence for both players in both profiles). Let (s_1, s_2) be an SPE of (Γ', α) which results in the consequence c and let (t_1, t_2) be an SPE of (Γ', β) which results in the consequence b. It must be that in α player 1 does not gain by switching to the strategy t_1 and thus the outcome of the play (t_1, s_2) must be c. Similarly, in β, player 2 does not gain by deviating to s_2 and thus it must be that the outcome of the play (t_1, s_2) is b, which is a contradiction.

Whereas I-implementation is not equivalent to SPE-implementation, we arrive at the following equivalence:

Proposition 2. *A social function f is guided-I-implementable if and only if it is SPE-implementable.*

Proof. By proposition 1 if f is guided-I-implementable then it is SPE-implementable. The proof in the other direction is straightforward: If we start with a game form Γ we employ the reduced normal form $G(\Gamma)$ and construct the guide starting from the end of the extensive game.

Remark. Proposition 2 sheds new light on Abreu and Matshushima [1] which uses I-implementation. As it turns out, the implementation of Abreu and Matshushima is actually guided-I-implementation and this explains the fact that Glazer and Perry [2] were able to find an analogous SPE-implementation.

References

1. D. Abreu and H. Matshushima, Virtual implementation in iteratively undominated strategy, *Econometrica* **60** (1992), 993–1008.
2. J. Glazer and M. Perry, Virtual implementation in backwards induction, *Games Econ. Behav.*, in press.
3. M. Herrero and S. Strivatsava, Implementation via backward induction, *J. Econ. Theory* **56** (1992), 70–88.
4. M. Jackson, Implementation of undominated strategies: A look at bounded mechanisms, *Rev. Econ. Stud.* **59** (1992), 757–776.
5. J. Moore and R. Rappulo, Subgame perfect implementation, *Econometrica* **56** (1988), 1191–1220.

Chapter 2

Motives and Implementation: On the Design of Mechanisms to Elicit Opinions*

Jacob Glazer[†] and Ariel Rubinstein[‡]

A number of experts receive noisy signals regarding a desirable public decision. The public target is to make the best possible decision on the basis of all the information available to the experts. We compare two "cultures": In the first, the experts are driven only by the public motive to choose the most desirable action. In the second, each expert is also driven by a private motive: to have his recommendation accepted. We show that in the first culture, every mechanism will have an equilibrium which does not achieve the public target, whereas the second culture gives rise to a mechanism whose unique equilibrium outcome does achieve the public target.

Journal of Economic Literature Classification Numbers: C72, D71.

1. Introduction

Motives are the basic building blocks of decision makers' preferences. For example, a parent's preferences in the selection of his child's school may combine educational, religious and social motives. A consumer's preferences in choosing what food to eat may involve the motives of taste, health and visual appearance. A voter's ranking of political candidates may be motivated by the candidates' views on security, foreign affairs, welfare, or perhaps their private lives.

---

*We wish to thank Dilip Abreu, Kyle Bagwell, Matt Jackson, Albert Ma, Tom Palfrey and Mike Riordan for comments on an earlier version of the paper and the Associate Editor of this journal for his encouragement.

[†]The Faculty of Management, Tel-Aviv University. E-mail: glazer@post.tau.ac.il.
 This author acknowledges financial support from the Israel Institute for Business Research.

[‡]The School of Economics, Tel-Aviv University and the Department of Economics, Princeton University. E-mail: rariel@post.tau.ac.il.
 This author acknowledges partial financial support from the United States-Israel Binational Science Foundation, Grant Number 1011-341.

We refer to a "culture" as the set of motives that drive the behavior of the individuals in a society. In some cultures, for example, the private life of a political candidate is an important issue for voters, while in others it is of no importance. Another example involves cultures in which voters are expected to consider only the "well-being of the nation" in contrast to others in which it is acceptable to take egoistic considerations into account as well. Although we often observe common motives among the members of a society, the weights assigned to each motive vary from one individual to another.

One approach to comparing one culture to another is to consider the morality of the motives involved in decision making. In contrast to this approach, we will be comparing cultures on the basis of implementability of the public target. Given a particular public target, we consider whether there is a mechanism that can attain the public target in a society where all individuals are guided only by the motives of the society's culture.

In our model, the decision whether to take a certain public action is made on the basis of the recommendations of a group of experts, each of whom possesses partial information as to which action is the socially desirable one. We have in mind situations such as the following: a group of referees who are to determine whether a paper is accepted or rejected, where each has an opinion regarding the acceptability of the paper; a decision whether or not to operate on a patient is made on the basis of consultations with several physicians; or an investigator who must determine whether or not a certain event has taken place, based on the evidence provided by a group of witnesses. In such scenarios, the agents may have different opinions, due to random elements that affect their judgment. The existence of such randomness is the rationale for making such decisions on the basis of more than one agent's opinion.

The public target (PT) is to take the best action, given the aggregation of all sincere opinions. To gain some intuition as to the difficulty in implementing the PT, consider a mechanism involving three experts who are asked to make simultaneous recommendations, where the alternative that receives the most votes is chosen. If all of the experts care only about attaining the PT, then this mechanism achieves the desired equilibrium, in which all the experts make sincere recommendations. However, other equilibria also exist, such as one in which all the experts recommend the same action, regardless of their actual opinion. This "bad" equilibrium is a reasonable possibility if each expert is also driven by a desire that his recommendation be accepted and even more so if the strategy to always recommend the same action regardless of the case, is less costly to an expert than the sincere recommendation strategy (which, for example, requires a referee to actually read the paper).

The objective of the paper is to compare between two cultures: one in which each expert is driven only by the public motive, i.e. he only wants to increase the probability that the right decision is made, and another in which an expert is also driven by a private motive, according to which he would like the public action to coincide with his recommendation. We find that in the former, the public target cannot be implemented and that every mechanism also has a bad equilibrium in which the probability of the right decision being made is not higher than in the case where only one expert is asked for his opinion. On the other hand, in the culture in which both motives exist, the social target is implementable: there exists a mechanism that attains only the desirable outcome regardless of the experts' tradeoff between the public and private motives.

The introduction of private motives is a departure from the standard implementation literature and can also be viewed as a critique of that literature. In the standard implementation problem, the designer is endowed with a set of consequences which he can use in the construction of the mechanism. The definition of a consequence does not include details of the events that take place during the play of the mechanism and the agents' preferences are defined only over those consequences. This is a particularly restrictive assumption whereby preferences are not sensitive to events that take place during the play of the mechanism. In the context of our model, for example, even if an expert is initially concerned only about the public target when asked to make a recommendation, he may also desire that his recommendation be accepted. The implementation literature ignores the possibility that such a motive will enter into an expert's considerations and treats the expert's moves during the play of the mechanism as meaningless messages.

Ignoring mechanism-related motives may yield misleading results. For example, consider the case in which a seller and a buyer evaluate an item with reservation values s and b, respectively. The designer wishes to implement the transfer of the good from the seller to the buyer at the price b as long as $b > s$. The standard implementation literature suggests that the seller makes a "take it or leave it offer" as a solution to this problem. However, this "solution" ignores the emotions aroused when playing the mechanism. A buyer may consider the offer of a price which leaves him with less than, say, 1% of the surplus, to be insulting. Although he may prefer getting 1% of the surplus to rejecting the transaction if it were offered by "nature", he would nevertheless prefer to reject an offer of 1% if made by the seller. The implementation literature might respond that the moves in a mechanism are abstract messages. However, the attractiveness of a mechanism should be judged, in our view, by its interpretation. The "take it or leave it" mechanism is attractive because the first move is interpreted as a price offer, rather than an abstract message.

Interestingly, the introduction of the private motive does not hamper the implementation of the PT and even facilitates it . This, however, does not diminish the significance of the critique: individuals are not indifferent to the content of the mechanism, as assumed by the standard implementation literature.

2. The Model

An action 0 or 1 is to be chosen. The desirable action depends on the state ω, which might be 0 or 1 with equal probabilities. The desirable action in state ω is ω. There is a set of agents $N = \{1, \ldots, n\}$ (n is odd and $n > 2$). Agent i receives a signal x_i, which in the state ω recieves the value ω with probability $1 > p > 1/2$ and the value $-\omega$ with probability $1 - p$ (we use the convention that $-1 = 0$ and $-0 = 1$). The signals are conditionally independent.

The number of 0s and 1s observed by the agents is the best information that can be collected in this situation. Note that in this model, no useful information is obtained if, for example, 10 signals are observed, 5 of which are 0s and 5 of which are 1s. In this case, the ex-post beliefs about the state remain identical to the ex-ante beliefs. This will not be the case under certain other informational structures, where such an outcome may signal the diminishing importance of the decision.

Denote by $V(K)$ the highest probability that the desirable action will be taken if a decision is made on the basis of the realization of K signals only. That is, for any given K agents,

$$V(K) = \text{prob}\{\text{strict majority of the } K \text{ agents get the right signal}\}$$
$$+ 1/2 \, \text{prob}\{\text{exactly one-half of the } K \text{ agents get the right signal}\}.$$

Note that $V(2k) = V(2k - 1)$ and $V(2k + 1) > V(2k)$. The fact that V is only weakly increasing is a special case of the observation made by Radner and Stiglitz (1984) that value of information functions are often not concave, that is, the marginal value of a signal is not decreasing in the number of signals. The equality $V(2k) = V(2k - 1)$ follows from our symmetry assumptions though it holds under less restrictive conditions as well (see Section 5 for a detailed discussion of this issue).

We define a *mechanism* as the operation of collecting information from the agents, calculating the consequence and executing it. We model a mechanism as a finite extensive game form with imperfect information (but no imperfect recall), with the n agents being the players, without chance players and with consequences being either 0 or 1.

The following are examples of mechanisms:

The direct simultaneous mechanism: All agents simultaneously make a recommendation, 0 or 1, and the majority determines the consequence.

The direct sequential mechanism: The agents move sequentially in a predetermined order. Each agent moves only once by announcing his recommendation; the majority determines the consequence.

The leader mechanism: In the first stage, agents $2, \ldots, n$ each simultaneously makes a recommendation of either 0 or 1, which are submitted to agent 1 (the "leader"), who makes the final recommendation which determines the consequence.

A mechanism together with the random elements define a Bayesian game form. Executing an n-tuple of strategies in a mechanism yields a lottery with the consequence 0 or 1.

The public target (PT) is to maximize π_1, the probability that the desirable action will be taken (i.e. the consequence ω in state ω). This definition assumes that the loss entailed in making the mistake of taking the action 0 at state 1 is the same as the loss entailed in making the mistake of taking the action 1 at state 0.

Each agent i can be driven by at most two motives: public and private. The public motive, which coincides with the PT, is to maximize π_1. The private motive is to maximize $\pi_{2,i}$, the probability that i's recommendation coincides with the consequence of the mechanism. In order to precisely define the private motive we add a profile of sets of histories $(R_i)_{i \in N}$ to the description of a mechanism so that R_i is interpreted as the set of histories in which agent i makes a recommendation. We require that for every $h \in R_i$, player i chooses between two actions 0 and 1, and that there is no terminal history h which has two subhistories in R_i.

When we say that agent i is driven only by the public motive, we mean that he wishes only to increase π_1. When we say that he is driven by both the private and the public motives we mean that he has certain preferences strictly increasing in both π_1 and $\pi_{2,i}$.

Our analysis ignores the existence of other private motives. For example, after the decision whether to operate on a patient is made, some additional information may be obtained that helps identify the right ex-post action. Then, a new motive may emerge: the desire of each physician to be proven ex-post right. We do not consider cultures with this motive and our analysis best fits situations in which the "truth" never becomes known.

The concept of equilibrium we adopt is sequential equilibrium in pure strategies (for simultaneous mechanisms this coincides with the Bayesian-Nash equilibrium). Given a profile of preferences over the public and private motives, we say that a mechanism implements the PT if in every sequential equilibrium of the game, $\pi_1 = V(n)$. That is, the consequence of any sequential equilibrium, for every profile of signals, is identical to the signal observed by the majority of agents.

3. The Impossibility of Implementation When All Agents are Driven by the Public Motive Only

In this section, we will show that if all agents are driven by the public motive only, there is no mechanism that implements the PT. That is, for any mechanism, the game obtained by the mechanism coupled with the agents' objective of increasing π_1 only, has a sequential equilibrium with $\pi_1 < V(n)$.

In order to achieve a better understanding of the difficulty in implementing the PT, we will first consider the three mechanisms described in the previous section and determine what it is about each that prevents "truth-telling" from being the only equilibrium. We say that an agent uses the "T" strategy if, whenever he makes a recommendation, it is identical to the signal he has received. "NT" is the strategy whereby an agent who has received the signal x recommends $-x$ and "c" ($c = 0, 1$) is the strategy whereby an agent announces c independently of the signal he has received.

The direct simultaneous mechanism: For this mechanism, all agents playing "T" is an equilibrium. However, the two equilibria proposed below do not yield the PT:

(1) All agents play "c" (since $n \geq 3$ a single deviation of agent i will not change π_1).

(2) Agents 1 and 2 play "0" and "1", respectively, while all other agents play "T".

One might argue that the equilibrium in which all agents play "T" is the most reasonable one since telling the truth is a natural focal mode of behavior. However, the notion of implementation which we use does not attribute any focal status to truth-telling. Note that although we do not include the cost of implementing a strategy in the model, one could conceive of costs associated with the strategies "T" or "NT", which could be avoided by executing "0" or "1". The existence of such costs makes the equilibrium in which all agents choose "c" quite stable: Executing the strategy "T" will not increase π_1 but will impose costs on the agent.

Note also that in this game the strategy "T" is not dominant (not even weakly so) when $n > 3$. For example, for $n = 5$, if agents 1 and 2 play "0", and agents 3 and 4 play "T", then "1" is a better strategy for agent 5 than "T". These strategies lead to different outcomes only when agents 3 and 4 get the signal 1 and agent 5 gets the signal 0. The strategy "1" is better than "T" for agent 5 in the event $\{\omega = 1$ and $(x_3, x_4, x_5) = (1, 1, 0)\}$ and is worse in the less likely event $\{\omega = 0$ and $(x_3, x_4, x_5) = (1, 1, 0)\}$.

The direct sequential mechanism: This mechanism does not implement the PT either. All agents playing "T" is an equilibrium. However, following are two other equilibria:

(1) Agent 1 plays "T" and all other agents match his recommendation with beliefs that assign no significance to any out-of-equilibrium moves. This is a sequential equilibrium with $\pi_1 = V(1)$.

(2) Agent 1 plays "NT", agents $2, \ldots, n - 1$ play "T", and agent n announces the opposite of what agent 1 has announced. This is a sequential equilibrium strategy profile with $\pi_1 = V(n - 2)$. Agent 1 cannot profitably deviate (since agent n neutralizes his vote in any case). Agent n cannot profitably deviate since if he conforms to the equilibrium, then $\pi_1 = V(n - 2)$, and if instead he plays "T", then π_1 will be even smaller. Note that this equilibrium does not have any out-of-equilibrium histories and thus cannot be excluded by any of the standard sequential equilibrium refinements.

The leader mechanism: Once again, there is an equilibrium with $\pi_1 = V(n)$. However, the following is a sequential equilibrium with $\pi_1 = V(1)$: agents $1, 2, , \ldots, n - 1$ play "0"; agent n, who is the leader, always announces his signal independently of the recommendations he receives from the agents and assigns no significance to deviations.

In all the above mechanisms there is an equilibrium which is optimal in the sense that it maximizes π_1 over all strategy profiles. This equilibrium strategy profile will emerge if each agent follows a general principle which calls on him to take his action in a profile that is both Pareto optimal and a Nash equilibrium, if such a profile exists. One might argue that this reduces the importance of the problem we are considering. We would disagree. First, on the basis of casual empirical observation we note that groups of experts are often "stuck" in bad equilibria. The reader will probably have little difficulty recalling cases in which he participated in a collective decision process and had a thought like the following: "There is no reason for me to seriously consider not supporting α, since everybody else is going to support α in any case." Second, note that even though an agent in this section is driven only by the public motive, we think about him as having another motive in the background: to reduce the complexity of executing his strategy. If agents put a relatively "small" weight on the complexity motive, truth-telling would remain a unique Pareto-optimal behavior, which is a Nash equilibrium. However, it is less obvious that an agent will indeed invoke this principle, since the complexity motive dictates against it.

The following proposition not only shows that there is no mechanism which implements the PT but also that every mechanism has a "bad" equilibrium with π_1 no larger than the probability that would obtain were a single agent nominated to make a decision based only on the signal he receives.

Proposition 1. *If all agents are only interested in increasing π_1, then every mechanism will have a sequential equilibrium with $\pi_1 \leq V(1)$.*

We first provide the intuition behind the proof.

Consider a one-stage, simultaneous-move mechanism. We construct a sequential equilibrium with $\pi_1 \leq V(1)$. If the outcome of the mechanism is constant, then the behavior of the agents is immaterial and $\pi_1 = V(0)$. Otherwise, there is an agent i and a profile of actions for the other agents $(a_j)_{j \neq i}$ so that the consequence of the mechanism is sensitive to agent i's action. That is, there are two actions, b_0 and b_1, for agent i that yield the consequences 0 and 1, respectively. Assign any agent $j \neq i$ to play the action a_j independently of the signal he has received. Assign agent i to play the action b_x if he has received the signal x. This profile of strategies yields $\pi_1 = V(1)$ and any deviation is unprofitable since although the outcome of the mechanism depends on at most two signals, we have $V(2) = V(1)$.

Now consider a two-stage mechanism in which all the agents make a move at each stage. We first construct the strategies for the second stage. For every profile of actions taken in the first stage, for which the consequence is not yet determined, assign strategies in a manner similar to the one used in the one-stage mechanism. We proceed by constructing the strategies for the first stage. If the outcome of the mechanism is always determined in the first stage, then the two-stage mechanism is essentially one stage, and we can adapt the sequential equilibrium constructed for the one-stage mechanism above. Otherwise, assign each agent i to play an action a_i^* in the first stage independently of his signal, where (a_i^*) is a profile of actions that does not determine the consequence of the mechanism. Coupling this with beliefs that do not assign any significance to deviations in the first stage, we obtain a sequential equilibrium with $\pi_1 = V(1)$.

Proof of Proposition 1. We provide a proof for the case in which the mechanism is one with perfect information and possibly simultaneous moves (see Osborne and Rubinstein (1994), page 102, for a definition). Though the proof does not cover the possibility of imperfect information, the definition of a game form with perfect information allows for several agents to move simultaneously. A history in such a game is an element of the type $(a^1, \ldots, a^K)$ where a^k is a profile of actions taken simultaneously by the agents in a set of agents denoted by $P(a^1, \ldots, a^{k-1})$.

For any given mechanism, we construct a sequential equilibrium with $\pi_1 \leq V(1)$. For any non-terminal history h, denote by $d(h)$ the maximal L, so that $(h, a^1, \ldots, a^L)$ is also a history. Let $(h^t)_{t=1,\ldots,T}$ be an ordering of the histories in the mechanism so that $d(h^t) \leq d(h^{t+1})$ for all t.

The equilibrium strategies are constructed inductively. At the t'th stage of the construction, we deal with the history $h^t = h$ (and some of its subhistories). If the strategies at history h have been determined in earlier stages, move on to the next stage; if not, two possible cases arise:

Case 1: There are two action profiles, a and b, in $A(h)$ and an agent $i^* \in P(h)$ such that $a_i = b_i$ for all $i \neq i^*$ and if the agents follow the strategies as previously defined, then the outcomes which follow histories (h, a) and (h, b) are 0 and 1, respectively.

In such a case, we continue as follows:

(i) For every $i \in P(h) - \{i^*\}$, assign the action a_i to history h independently of the signal that i observes; for agent i^*, assign the action a_i^* (b_i^*) if his signal is 0 (1).

(ii) If h' is a proper subhistory of h and the strategy profile for h' was not defined earlier, assign to any $i \in P(h')$ the action a_i , where (h', a) is a subhistory of h as well (that is, the agents in $P(h')$ move towards h).

Case 2: If for every $a, b \in A(h)$ the outcome of the game is the same if the agents follow the strategies after (h, a) and (h, b), then pick an arbitrary $a^* \in A(h)$ and assign the action a_i^* to each $i \in P(h)$ independently of their signal.

Beliefs are updated according to the strategies. Whenever an out-of-equilibrium event occurs, the agents continue to hold their initial beliefs.

We now show that we have indeed constructed a sequential equilibrium. Note that for every history h, there is at most one agent whose equilibrium behavior in the game following h depends on his own signal. If the outcome of the subgame starting at h depends on the moves of one of the players, then all players at h will still hold their initial beliefs and a unilateral deviation cannot increase π_1 beyond $V(2) = V(1)$.

The extension of the proof to the case of imperfect information requires a somewhat more delicate construction in order to fulfill the requirement that the same action be assigned to all histories in the same information set.   □

Virtual Implementation

Virtual Bayesian Nash implementation of the PT may be possible. Abreu and Matsushima (1992) suggest a direct simultaneous mechanism according to which the outcome is determined with probability $1 - \varepsilon$ by the majority of announcements and with probability ε/n by agent i's recommendation $(i = 1, \ldots, n)$. This mechanism requires the use of random devices and allows for the unsound possibility that although $n - 1$ agents observe and report the signal 0, the outcome is 1.

Related Literature

Up to this point, the analysis is a standard investigation of a problem of sequential equilibrium implementation with imperfect information (see Moore (1992) and Palfrey (1992)). A related model is Example 2 in Palfrey and Srivastava (1989) which differs from ours in that each agent in their model prefers that the social action coincide with the signal he has received. Both models demonstrate the limits of Bayesian implementation. Proposition 1 is related to results presented in Jackson (1991), which provided both a necessary condition and a sufficient condition for Bayesian implementation using simultaneous mechanisms. The PT in our model does not satisfy Bayesian monotonicity, which is a necessary condition for such implementation. Proposition 1 does not follow from Jackson's results since we relate to extensive mechanisms in addition to simultaneous ones.

4. Implementation is Possible When All Agents are Driven by Both Motives

We now move from the culture in which all agents are driven only by the public motive to one in which they are driven by both the public and private motives. We show that in this case implementation of the PT is possible.

The mechanism we propose is as follows: Agent 1 is assigned the special status of "controller". In the first stage, each agent, except the controller, secretly makes a recommendation while the controller simultaneously determines a set of agents S whose votes will be counted. The set S must be even-numbered (and may be empty) and must not include the controller. In the second stage, the controller learns the result of the votes cast by the members of S and only then adds his vote. The majority of the votes in $S \cup \{1\}$ determines the outcome.

Following are three points to note about this mechanism:

(1) The controller has a double role. First, he has the power to discard the votes of those agents who play a strategy that negatively affects π_1. Second, he contributes his own view whenever his vote is pivotal.

(2) Each agent (except the controller) makes a recommendation in the first stage even if his vote is not counted. An agent whose vote is not counted is driven only by the private motive and hence will vote honestly if he believes that the outcome of the mechanism will be positively correlated with the signal he receives.

(3) Whenever the controller is pivotal, his recommendation will be the outcome; when he is not, he does not reduce π_1 by joining the majority. Thus, the mechanism is such that the private motive of the controller never conflicts with his public motive.

We will prove that this mechanism implements the PT for every profile of preferences in which the agents are driven by both the public and private motives (independently of the weights they assign to the two motives as long as both weights are positive). For every game induced by the mechanism and a profile of such preferences, the only equilibrium is one in which all agents other than the controller play "T" in the first stage and they are all included in S, and the controller joins the majority in S in the second stage unless he is pivotal, in which case he plays "T".

Proposition 2. *The following mechanism implements the PT for any profile of preferences that satisfies the condition that each agent i's preferences increase in both π_1 and $\pi_{2,i}$.*

Stage 1: All the agents, except agent 1, simultaneously make a recommendation of either 0 or 1, while agent 1 announces an even-numbered set of agents, S, which does not include himself.

Stage 2: Agent 1 is informed about the total number of members in S who voted 1 and makes his own recommendation of either 0 or 1.

The majority of votes among $S \cup \{1\}$ determines the consequence.

Following are the main arguments to prove that no other equilibria are possible:

(1) The controller's decision whether to include in S an agent who plays "NT" is the result of two considerations: the information he obtains from such an agent, and the fact that this agent's vote negatively affects the outcome. We will show that the latter is a stronger consideration and therefore, agents who play "NT" are excluded from S.

(2) Since the mechanism enables the controller to maximize the public motive without worrying about the private motive, he selects the set S so as to be the "most informative". Thus, the set S consists of all agents who play "T" and possibly some agents who play "0" or "1" (the difference between the number of "0"s and the number of "1"s cannot exceed 1).

(3) There is no equilibrium in which some of the agents in S choose a pooling strategy ("c"), since one of them increases $\pi_{2,i}$ without decreasing π_1 by switching to "T".

(4) There is no equilibrium with $S \neq N - \{1\}$. If agent i is excluded from S, then by (2) he does not play "T", but since he does not affect the consequence and since in equilibrium $\pi_1 > 1/2$, he can profitably deviate to "T" and thereby increase $\pi_{2,i}$.

Note that for the mechanism to work, it is important that the controller only learns the result of the votes in S and not how each agent voted. In order to see why, assume that $n = 3$ and agent 1 receives the additional information of how each agent voted. The following is a sequential equilibrium with $\pi_1 < V(3)$: In the first stage, agent 1 chooses $S = \{2,3\}$, agent 2 plays "0" and agent 3 plays "T". In the second stage, agent 1 plays "T" in the case that agents 2 and 3 voted 0 and 1, respectively and plays "0" in the case that agents 2 and 3 voted 1 and 0, respectively. This strategy profile is supported by out-of-equilibrium beliefs that a vote 1 by agent 2 means that he received the signal 0. This is not an equilibrium in our proposed mechanism since in the second stage agent 1 cannot distinguish between the two profiles of votes $(1,0)$ and $(0,1)$.

Note that the role of the controller in the first stage of the mechanism is somewhat similar to the role of the "stool pigeon" in Palfrey (1992) and Baliga (1994). The stool pigeon is an agent appended to the mechanism whose role, as described by Palfrey (1992), is "...to eliminate unwanted equilibria because, while he does not know the types of his opponents, he can perfectly predict their strategies, as always assumed in equilibrium analysis." In a previous version of the paper we showed that Proposition 1 is still valid when the use of a stool pigeon is allowed. The mechanism of Proposition 2 "works" because all agents are also driven by the private motive.

Proof of Proposition 2. The following is an equilibrium with $\pi_1 = V(n)$. In the first stage, agent 1 chooses $S = N - \{1\}$ and all agents in $N - \{1\}$ play "T". In the second stage, if more agents recommend x than $-x$, then agent 1 votes x; in the case of a tie, agent 1 plays "T".

In order to prove that this is the only sequential equilibrium, the following five lemmas will be useful:

Denote by $\pi_1(s_1, \ldots, s_K)$ the probability that the majority recommends the correct action in the simultaneous game with K (an odd integer) players who use the strategies $(s_1, \ldots, s_K)$ and let $\pi_{2,i}(s_1, \ldots, s_K)$ be the probability that i's recommendation will coincide with the majority's recommendation. Then:

Lemma 1. *If* $\pi_1(s_1, \ldots, s_K, NT, T) \geq p$ *then* $\pi_1(s_1, \ldots, s_K, NT, T) < \pi_1(s_1, \ldots, s_K)$ *(i.e. eliminating a pair of agents, one of whom plays "T" and one of whom plays "NT", increases π_1).*

Lemma 2. *If* $s_i \neq T$ *for* $i = 1, \ldots, K$, *then* $\pi_1(s_1, \ldots, s_K) \leq 1/2$ *(i.e. if all agents play a constant strategy or "NT", then the probability that the majority will be correct cannot exceed $1/2$).*

Lemma 3. $\pi_1(0,0,0,\ldots,0,T\ldots T) < \pi_1(0,\ldots,0,T\ldots T)$ *(i.e. if all agents play 0 or "T", then eliminating two agents who play "0" increases π_1).*

Lemma 4. $\pi_1(T,T\ldots T) > \pi_1(0,T,\ldots,T)$ *and* $\pi_{2,1}(T,T\ldots T) > \pi_{2,1}(0,T,\ldots,T)$ *(if all other agents play "T", then an agent i who plays "0" improves π_1 and $\pi_{2,i}$ by switching to "T").*

Lemma 5. $\pi_1(T,1,T\ldots T) = \pi_1(0,1,T,\ldots,T,T)$ *and* $\pi_{2,1}(T,1,T\ldots T) > \pi_{2,1}(0,1,\ldots,T,T) = 1/2$ *(i.e. if one agent plays "0", another agent plays "1" and all other agents play "T" then the "0" agent will not hurt the PT by instead playing "T" and will improve his π_i).*

Note that the value of π_1 in the game induced by our mechanism, i.e. when agent 1 selects some set of agents S (and his strategy in the second stage may depend on the recommendation of the majority of members of S), is the same as the value of π_1 in the simultaneous game with the set of agents $S \cup \{1\}$ where agent 1 plays his component of the strategy conditional on a tie in the recommendations of the agents in S.

In any equilibrium, it must be that $\pi_1(s_1,\ldots,s_n) \geq p$ since agent 1 can obtain $\pi_{2,1} = 1$ and $\pi_1 = p$ by selecting $S = \emptyset$.

By Lemmas 1 and 2, $\pi_1(s_1,\ldots,s_K) < p$ if the number of players in the profile $(s_1,\ldots,s_K)$ who play "NT" is as large as the number of players in the profile who play "T". Therefore, in every equilibrium, the number of agents in S who play "NT" cannot be strictly larger than the number of agents who play "T".

Thus, by Lemma 1, if there is an agent in S who plays "NT", agent 1 will improve π_1 by eliminating a pair of agents, one of whom plays "NT" and one of whom plays "T". Therefore, none of the agents in the selected S plays "NT".

By Lemma 3, the number of agents who play "c" differs by at most 1 from the number of agents who play "$-c$".

Assume, without loss of generality, that the number of agents in S who play "0" is at least as high as the number of agents in S who play "1".

If the number of agents in S who play "0" is the same as the number of agents who play "1", then agent 1 must play "T" and then by Lemma 5 any such agent would do better by switching to "T".

If the number of agents in S who play "0" is larger by one than the number of agents in S who play "1", then agent 1 must play either "T" or "1" and then by either Lemma 4 or Lemma 5 any agent who plays "0" will do better by switching to "T".

Thus, in equilibrium, all agents in S play "T" and agent 1 plays "T" in the case of a tie. Thus, any agent i outside of S will also play "T" (in order to maximize his $\pi_{2,i}$) and it is optimal for agent 1 to choose $S = N - \{1\}$.

Comment: The Culture with Only the Private Motive

Implementation of the PT is impossible in the culture in which all agents are driven only by the private motive, that is, when each agent i is interested only in increasing $\pi_{2,i}$. In fact, implementation of the PT is impossible in any culture in which all motives are independent of the state. The reason for this is that in such a culture, whatever the mechanism is, if $\sigma = (\sigma_{i,x})$ is a sequential equilibrium strategy profile (i.e. $\sigma_{i,x}$ is i's strategy given that he observes the signal x), then the strategy profile σ' where $\sigma'_{i,x} = \sigma_{i,-x}$ (i.e. each agent who receives the signal x plays as if he had received the signal $-x$) is also a sequential equilibrium strategy profile. Thus, the outcome of σ when all agents receive the signal 1 is the same as the outcome of σ' when all agents receive the signal 0, and thus one of them does not yield the PT.

5. A Discussion of the Symmetry Assumption

One might suspect that symmetry plays a crucial role in obtaining Proposition 1, the springboard of the analysis. Indeed several symmetry conditions are imposed: the two states are equally likely; the loss from taking the action 1 when the state is 0 is equal to the loss from taking the action 0 when the state is 1; the signal random variable is the same for all agents; and the probability that the signal is correct, given the state, is independent of the state.

Furthermore, one or more "deviations" from the symmetry assumptions invalidates Proposition 1. Assume that the probability of state 0 is "slightly" larger than the probability of state 1. In this case, $V(2) > V(1) > V(0)$. It is easy to verify that the following simultaneous mechanism implements the PT for the case in which there are two agents driven by the public motive only:

	a	b	c
a	0	0	1
b	0	1	0
c	1	0	0

The example demonstrates that the key element in the proof of the non-implementability of the PT in the culture with only the public motive is that $V(2) = V(1)$, an equality that follows from the symmetry assumptions. Thus, one might suspect that we are dealing with a "razor-edged" case.

We have three responses:

1. Deviations from the symmetry assumptions will not necessarily make the PT implementable when all agents are driven by the public motive only. Following are two examples with $n = 3$ for simplicity:

    (a) Assume that β, the probability of state 1, is such that only if all three agents receive the signal 0, does it become more likely that the state is indeed 0 (i.e., $[p/(1-p)]^3 > \beta/(1-\beta) > [p/(1-p)]^2$). In this case, $V(0) > V(2) = V(1)$ and the PT is not implementable.

    (b) Assume that the signals observed by the three agents are not equally informative. Denote by p_i the probability that agent i in state ω receives the signal ω. Assume that $p_1 > p_2 = p_3 > 1/2$ and that it is optimal not to follow agent 1's signal only if the signal observed by both agents 2 and 3 is the opposite of the one observed by agent 1. In that case, it is easy to see that any mechanism has an equilibrium with $\pi_1 = p_1 < V(3)$.

    In fact, it can be shown that in every situation where there is a number $k < n$ for which $V(K) = V(K+1)$ but $V(K) < V(n)$, the PT is not implementable when agents are driven by the public motive only.

2. The main ideas of the paper are also relevant in the asymmetric cases in which V is strictly increasing. Note that in the background of our model one can imagine an additional cost imposed on an agent who executes a strategy that requires him to actually observe the signal before making a recommendation. Denote this cost by γ. Let m^* be the solution of $\max_{m \leq n} V(m) - m\gamma$. In other words, m^* is the "socially optimal" number of active agents. Even when it is strictly increasing, the function V is typically not concave. Hence, it is possible that there is an $m \leq m^*$ so that $V(m) - V(m-1) < \gamma$. In such a case, the PT is not implementable when agents are driven by the public motive only. The key point is that if $m-1$ agents seek to increase π_1, the marginal contribution of the m'th agent will be less than the cost he incurs.

3. Finally, we disagree with the claim that symmetric cases are "zero-probability events". The symmetric case is important even if the number 0.5 has measure 0 in the unit interval. Asymmetric models have a special status since they fit situations in which all individuals cognitively ignore asymmetries.

References

Abreu, D. and H. Matsushima (1992), "Virtual Implementation in Iteratively Undominated Strategies: Complete Information", *Econometrica, 60,* 993–1008.

Baliga, S. (1996) "The Not-So-Secret-Agent: Implementation and Professional Monitors," mimeo, Kellogg GSM (M.E.D.S.), Northwestern University.

Jackson, M. (1991), "Bayesian Implementation", *Econometrica, 59,* 461–478.

Moore, J. (1992), "Implementation, Contracts, and Renegotiation in Environments with Complete Information", in J.J. Laffont (editor), *Advances in Economic Theory: Sixth World Congress Volume I,* Cambridge University Press, pp. 182–282.

Osborne, M. and A. Rubinstein (1994), *A Course in Game Theory,* MIT Press.

Palfrey, T. (1992), "Implementation in Bayesian Equilibrium: the Multiple Equilibrium Problem in Mechanism Design", in J.J. Laffont (editor), *Advances in Economic Theory: Sixth World Congress Volume I,* Cambridge University Press, pp. 283–323.

Palfrey,T. and S. Srivastava (1989), "Mechanism Design with Incomplete Information: A Solution to the Implementation Problem", *Journal of Political Economy, 97,* 668–691.

Radner, R. and J. Stiglitz (1984), "A Nonconcavity in the Value of Information", in *Bayesian Models in Economic Theory,* M. Boyer and R.E. Kihlstrom (eds.), Elsevier Science Publishers, Chapter 3.

Chapter 3

Debates and Decisions: On a Rationale of Argumentation Rules

Jacob Glazer

The Faculty of Management, Tel Aviv University, Tel Aviv, Israel

Ariel Rubinstein*

The School of Economics, Tel Aviv University, Israel
and
Department of Economics, Princeton University,
Princeton, New Jersey

We view a debate as a mechanism by which an uninformed decision maker (the listener) extracts information from two informed debaters, who hold contradicting positions regarding the right decision. During the debate, the debaters raise arguments and, based on these arguments, the listener reaches a conclusion. Using a simple example, we investigate the mechanism design problem of constructing rules of debate that maximize the probability that the listener reaches the right conclusion, subject to constraints on the form and length of the debate. It is shown that optimal debate rules have the property that the conclusion drawn by the listener is not necessarily the same as the conclusion he would have drawn, had he interpreted the information revealed to him or her during the debate literally. The optimal design of debate rules requires that the information elicited from a counterargument depends on the argument it counterargues. We also link our discussion with the pragmatics literature.

Journal of Economic Literature Classification Numbers: C72, D78.

1. Introduction

This paper is a part of our long-term research agenda for studying different aspects of debates using game theoretic tools. Debates are common phenomena in our daily life. In a debate, two or more parties (the debaters), who disagree regarding some issue, raise arguments to support their

---

*Most of this author's research was conducted while he was a visiting scholar at the Russell Sage Foundation, New York during the academic year 1996–97.

positions or to rebuff the other party's arguments. Sometimes the purpose of the debaters is to argue just for the sake of arguing, and sometimes their aim is to try to convince the other party to change his position. In this paper, however, the debaters argue in front of a third party (the listener) each trying to persuade the listener to support his position. Note that a debate is different from bargaining and war, which are also mechanisms for conflict resolutions, in that the outcome of those mechanisms heavily depends on the rivals' power. A debate is different from a conversation, which is also a mechanism in which interested parties make arguments, in that in a conversation, there is a common interest among the parties.

We view a debate as a mechanism by which an uninformed decision-maker (the listener) extracts information from two informed parties (the debaters). The debaters hold contradicting positions about the decision that should be made. The right conclusion depends on the realization of several aspects. During the debate the debaters raise arguments to support their respective positions and on the basis of these arguments, the listener reaches a conclusion regarding the right decision. When we say that a debater raises the argument x, we mean that he reveals that the realization of aspect x supports his position. When the other debater responds to an argument x with an argument y, we refer to argument y as a counterargument. The realizations of the aspects are assumed to be independent. All aspects are assumed to be equally weighted, in the sense that all of them have the same value of information regarding the right decision.

Under the above assumptions one may expect the optimal debate conclusion to be a function only of the number of arguments made by each party. Our intuition supported by some experimental evidence is that this is not correct: after one argument has been made by one party, the subjects, in the role of the other party, may find the seemingly equal counterarguments unequally persuasive. We analyze the optimal debate rules using a simple example. We show that the optimal debate rules have the property that the strength of a counterargument may depend on the argument it is countering, even when there is no informational dependency between the two arguments. In particular, we show the invalidity of the following principle, regarding the dependency of the outcome of a debate on the argument raised by one debater and the counterargument raised by the other debater:

THE DEBATE CONSISTENCY (DC) PRINCIPLE:. It is impossible that "x wins the debate" if y is brought up as a counterargument to x, but "y wins the debate" if x is brought up as a counterargument to y.

We show that this principle is *not* necessarily a property of debate rules optimally designed to extract information from the debaters.

Let us emphasize that we do not intend to provide a general theory of debates. Our only aim is to point out that the logic of the optimal design of debate rules is subtle and contains some features which are not intuitive.

2. Motivating Examples

Before we proceed to the model we will discuss two examples to demonstrate our intuition regarding the subtle nature of what people perceive as a good counterargument.

QUESTION 1. You are participating in a public debate about the level of education in the world's capitals. You are trying to convince the audience that in most capital cities, the level of education has risen recently. Someone is challenging you, bringing up indisputable evidence showing that the level of education in *Bangkok* has deteriorated. Now it is your turn to respond. You have similar, indisputable evidence to show that the level of education in *Mexico City, Manila, Cairo*, and *Brussels* has gone up. However, because of time constraints, you can argue and present evidence only about one of the four cities mentioned above. Which city would you choose for making the strongest counterargument against *Bangkok*?

Our intuition is that in this debate scenario a good counterargument will be "close" to the argument it is countering, even though the geographical proximity is irrelevant to the substance of the arguments. Therefore we expect that most people will find the evidence about Manila to be a better counterargument than that about Mexico City, Cairo, or Brussels for rebuffing the evidence from Bangkok.

To support our intuition we presented the scenarios (described in Hebrew) to groups of subjects, students at Tel Aviv University. More experimental research is needed to establish our intuition as experimental observations, but we think that the results are of interest. A group of 38 subjects received the question and 50% of them agreed with our intuition and answered Manila. Each of the other alternatives was chosen by 21% of the students or less. A second group of 62 subjects was presented with Question 1 with the modification that Bangkok was replaced by Amsterdam. Here 78% of the subjects found Brussels the most persuasive counterargument against Amsterdam.

To prevent a possible claim that the above phenomenon is confined to cases where the subjects have some implicit beliefs about correlation between the arguments, we presented another group of subjects with the following question:

QUESTION 2. Two TV channels provide fixed program schedules for the five weekdays. You and a friend are debating which is the better channel before a third party. Your opponent argues in favor of channel A while you argue in favor of channel B. Both of you have access to the same five reports prepared by a highly respected expert, each of which refers to a different day of the week and recommends the better channel for that day. Your opponent begins the debate by quoting *Tuesday's* report, which found channel A's programs to be better. The listener then stops your opponent, asking you to reply. Both *Wednesday's* and *Thursday's* reports are in your favor; namely, they found channel B to be superior. However, you have time to present only one of these expert reports as a counterargument, after which the third party will make up his mind. Will you choose Wednesday or Thursday as a better counterargument to Tuesday?

About 69% of the 58 subjects found Wednesday, rather than Thursday, a better counterargument to Tuesday.

A puzzling element emerges from considering these examples. If two arguments contain the same quality of information, why is one of them considered to be a stronger counterargument than the other? The fact that Manila is closer to Bangkok than it is to Mexico City seems irrelevant to the substance of the debate, and yet it appears to dramatically affect the choice of a counterargument. Similarly, Wednesday is not a more significant day than Thursday in regard to the TV schedule, and yet it is assessed as a better counterargument against Tuesday.

One may view this phenomenon as a rhetoric fallacy. We, however, suggest another view. The logic of debate mechanisms, optimally designed to extract information from the debaters, may be quite subtle. The strength of an argument made by one debater may depend on the argument made by the other debater even when no informational dependencies exist between the arguments.

3. A Model

A decision-maker, called *the listener*, has to choose between two *outcomes*, O_1 and O_2. The "correct" outcome, from the point of view of the listener, depends on the realization of five *aspects*, numbered $1, \ldots, 5$. An aspect i may get one of two *values*, 1 or 2, with the interpretation that if it gets the value j, aspect i is evidence that supports the outcome O_j. A *state* is a five-tuple of 1's and 2's which describes the realizations of the five aspects. Let ω_j denote the value of aspect j at state ω. Let $i(\omega) = \{j|\omega_j = i\}$ be the set of aspects which support O_i, and denote by $n_i(\omega)$ the size of $i(\omega)$. The listener objective is to choose the outcome supported by the majority of arguments. For each state ω, denote by $C(\omega)$ the O_i, for which $n_i(\omega) \geq 3$; we will refer to $C(\omega)$ as the *correct* outcome at ω.

The listener is ignorant of the state. Two agents, called *debater* 1 and *debater* 2, have full information about the state. The preferences of the debaters are different from those of the listener. Each debater i prefers that outcome O_i will be chosen, regardless of the state.

We view a debate mechanism as a process in which each debater reveals pieces of information in order to persuade the listener to choose the outcome he (the debater) prefers. We model a debate as a combination of two elements:

procedural rules, which specify which order and what sort of arguments each debater is allowed to raise,

a *persuasion rule*, which specifies the relationship between the arguments presented in the debate and the outcome chosen by the listener.

We impose some constraints on the feasible debate mechanisms. Our first constraint is that the only moves a debater can make are to raise arguments that support his preferred outcome; that is, the set of feasible moves of debater i at the state ω is $i(\omega)$, where the move "j" is interpreted as the *argument*: "aspect j is in my favor." There are, in fact, three assumptions implicit in this constraint: First, debaters cannot make any moves other than raising arguments. Second, a debater cannot lie; namely, debater i cannot claim that the value of aspect j is i unless it is indeed i. Third, a debater cannot raise arguments that support the outcome preferred by the other debater. When debater i makes an argument and then debater j makes an argument, in sequence, we will refer to debater j's argument as a *counterargument*.

The second constraint concerns the complexity of the debate. Of course, if a debate in which all five aspects could be revealed was feasible, the correct outcome would be obtained with certainty. The listener could simply ask one of the debaters to make three arguments, and if that debater was able to fulfill this task, his preferred outcome would be chosen. However, we take the view that debate rules are affected not only by the goal of obtaining a good outcome, but also by the existence of constraints on the length and complexity of the debate. We define a debate as follows:

We find it suitable to model a *debate* as an extensive game form of one of three types:

(1) one-speaker debate: *one of the debaters* has to choose two arguments;
(2) simultaneous debate: the two debaters move *simultaneously*, each one has to make one argument;
(3) sequential debate: a *two-stage* game; at the first stage, one of the debaters has to choose one argument and at the second stage the other debater has to make one argument.

An outcome, O_1 or O_2, is attached to each terminal history. The attachment of an outcome to a terminal history is the *persuasion rule*.

Note that a debate is *not* the game form that will be actually played, as at each state the debaters are not allowed to make false arguments. A debate Γ will induce at each state ω a distinct game $\Gamma(\omega)$, played by the two debaters. The game form of the game $\Gamma(\omega)$ is obtained from Γ by deleting, for each debater i, all moves that are not in $i(\omega)$. If player i has to move after a history h, and at ω none of the arguments he is allowed to make at h is in $i(\omega)$, then we make the history h in the game $\Gamma(\omega)$ a terminal history and attach to h the outcome O_j (debater i looses). As to the preferences of each debater i in $\Gamma(\omega)$, we assume that debater i strictly prefers O_i to O_j independently of ω.

To clarify our construction consider, for example, the simultaneous debate. In a simultaneous debate Γ each player has five choices. The game form Γ specifies for each pair of choices, one for player 1 and one for player 2, an outcome, O_1 or O_2. (Actually the assignment of outcomes for the five pairs (t, t) is redundant.) At the state $\omega = (1, 1, 2, 2, 1)$, for example, the game $\Gamma(\omega)$ is a 3×2 game, where player 1 has to choose between arguments 1, 2, and 5 and player 2 has to choose between arguments 3 and 4. The outcome attached to each pair of moves in $\Gamma(\omega)$ is the outcome attached by the game form Γ.

Note the difference between our modeling and that of the standard implementation literature. In both cases the designer determines a game form and the state determines the game played at that state. In the standard implementation literature, the state is a profile of preference relations and the game form played at each state is fixed. In our framework, the preference relations are fixed and the game form varies with the state.

The game $\Gamma(\omega)$ is a zero-sum game and has a value, $v(\Gamma, \omega)$, which is a *lottery* over the set of outcomes. Let $m(\Gamma, \omega)$ be the probability that $v(\Gamma, \omega)$ assigns to the incorrect outcome. When $m(\Gamma, \omega) = 1$ we say that the debate Γ induces a *mistake* in the state ω.

Note that in simultaneous debates, $m(\Gamma, \omega)$ may get a value that is neither 0 nor 1. Consider, for example, the simultaneous debate Γ with the persuasion rule according to which debater 1 wins if and only if he argues for some i, and debater 2 does not argue for either $i + 1 \pmod 5$ or $i - 1$ $\pmod 5$. For the state $\omega = (1, 1, 2, 2, 2)$, the game $\Gamma(\omega)$ does not have a pure Nash equilibrium; the value of this game is O_i with probability $\frac{1}{2}$, for $i = 1, 2$ and $m(\Gamma, \omega) = \frac{1}{2}$.

All mistakes are weighted equally. An *optimal debate* is one that minimizes

$$m(\Gamma) = \sum_\omega m(\Gamma, \omega).$$

Note that we confined ourselves to the simplest example that could demonstrate our point. We needed two arguments in order to create at least the possibility for a debate. We found the case of three aspects uninteresting, as the optimal debate would be the one where only one speaker is required to raise two arguments in order to win. As we are not interested in actually designing optimal debates but only in investigating the logic of debates, we make do with investigating the case of five aspects.

4. Analysis

Main Claim. Every optimal debate procedure is sequential and violates the DC principle.

The proof of the main claim is accomplished by analyzing the three possible persuasion rules:

4.1. *Only One Debator Is Allowed to Speak*

We start with the procedural rule where only one debater, say, debater 1, is allowed to present two arguments, after which an outcome is chosen. A persuasion rule here can be presented as a set of pairs of arguments, where the presentation of one of these pairs is necessary and sufficient for debater 1 to win. For example, the listener may be persuaded by any two arguments that support debater 1's position: This persuasion rule induces 10 mistakes (all states ω where $n_t(\omega) = 2$). A more interesting persuasion rule is one where the listener is persuaded by debater 1 only if the debater can present two arguments referring to two successive aspects. Here, the number of mistakes is five, four in favor of debater 1, and one in favor of debater 2 (in the state where aspects 1, 3, and 5 support debater 1). But we can do a bit better:

Claim 1. The minimal $m(\Gamma)$ for debates in which only one debater speaks is four. The only debate (up to a permutation of the names of the arguments and the identity of the speaker) which induces four mistakes is the one where the speaker is persuasive if and only if he presents two arguments from either $\{1, 2, 3\}$ or $\{4, 5\}$.

Proof.   A debate in which only debater 1 speaks is characterized by a set E of sets of size 2, so that debater 1 wins in every ω in which his set of arguments, $1(\omega)$, contains a set in E. Any $e \in E$ produces one mistake in the state ω in which $1(\omega) = e$.   □

Consider the debate where debater 1 has to show two arguments regarding aspects which are in either $\{1, 2, 3\}$ or $\{4, 5\}$ (that is, $E = \{\{1, 2\}, \{2, 3\}, \{1, 3\}, \{4, 5\}\}$). This debate induces four mistakes in favor of 1 and none in favor of 2 (if $n_1(\omega) \geq 3$, then there must be at least two aspects supporting 1, either in the set $\{1, 2, 3\}$ or in the set $\{4, 5\}$).

To see that there is no one-speaker debate with less than four mistakes, and that the one above is the unique optimal one-speaker debate (up to a permutation of the names of the arguments and the identity of the speaker), consider a one-speaker debate that induces at most four mistakes. Each aspect must appear in one of the sets in E since otherwise there are at least six mistakes. It must be that the set E is such that one of the aspects, let us say 1, appears in at most one set of E, let us say $\{1, 2\}$. For each $\{i, j\} \subseteq \{3, 4, 5\}$, either $\{i, j\}$ is in E and there is a mistake in the state ω in which $1(\omega) = \{i, j\}$ and if not there is a mistake in the state ω in which $1(\omega) = \{1, i, j\}$. Neither $\{2, i\}$ nor $\{2, j\}$ is in E since it would induce a fifth mistake. Thus, if $\{i, j\}$ is not in E there will be one additional mistake in the state ω in which $1(\omega) = \{2, i, j\}$. We conclude that it must be that $E = \{\{1, 2\}, \{3, 4\}, \{3, 5\}, \{4, 5\}\}$.

4.2. *Simultaneous Debates*

Claim 2. The minimal $m(\Gamma)$ for simultaneous debates is five.

Proof.   A simultaneous debate specifies an outcome, $O(x, y)$, to be chosen if debater 1 makes the argument x and debater 2 argues y. Consider the debate Γ, in which $O(x,y) = O_2$ if and only if $y = x + 1 \pmod 5$ or $y = x - 1 \pmod 5$. We will see that $m(\Gamma) = 5$. Debater 1 rightly wins in any state ω where $1(\omega)$ contains three successive aspects (ordered on a circle), and he rightly loses in any state where $1(\omega)$ contains zero, one, or exactly two non-consecutive arguments. We are left with 10 states, in 5 of which $1(\omega)$ contain three non-successive aspects (e.g., (1,1,2,1,2)). In the other 5 states, there are precisely two aspects in favor of debater 1 and they are successive (e.g., (1,1,2,2,2)). In each of these 10 states, the value of the induced game is the lottery that selects the two outcomes equally. Thus, $m(\Gamma) = 10(\frac{1}{2}) = 5$. $\qquad\square$

We will now show that $m(\Gamma) \geq 5$ for any simultaneous debate Γ. For a given aspect x, let v_x be the number of y's so that $O(x,y) = O_1$ and, similarly, for a given aspect y, let w_y be the number of x's so that $O(x,y) = O_2$. Of course, $\sum_x v_x + \sum_y w_y = 20$.

If, for some x, $v_x = 4$, debater 1 wins at any state ω with $\omega_x = 1$; hence, at least five mistakes are induced. Similarly, if for some y, $w_y = 4$, there will be five mistakes induced. Thus, assume that $v_x \leq 3$ for all x and $w_y \leq 3$ for all y. Consider the set Ω' consisting of the 20 states, ω, for which $n_1(\omega)$ is 2 or 3. We will see that $\sum_{\omega \in \Omega'} m(\Gamma, \omega) \geq 5$. For a state ω with $n_1(\omega) = 2$, the induced game $\Gamma(\omega)$ is a 2×3 game and the correct outcome is O_2. The value of $\Gamma(\omega)$ will be O_2 with probability 1 only if there is a column (a winning strategy) that guarantees debater 2's victory. A similar argument can be made for a state ω with $n_1(\omega) = 3$. Otherwise, $\omega \in \Omega'$ contributes at least $\frac{1}{2}$ to $m(\Gamma)$.

If $v_x = 1$, then x will never be a winning strategy in any of the 20 games. If $v_x = 2$, the action x can be used by debater 1 as a winning strategy in exactly one induced 3×2 game. If $v_x = 3$, the strategy x can be used by debater 1 to win in three 3×2 games, but it will also allow him to win wrongly in one 2×3 game. Thus, given any vector $(v_1, \ldots, v_5, w_1, \ldots, w_5)$, any state ω with $\omega(1)$ equaling 2 or 3 will contribute $\frac{1}{2}$ to $m(\Gamma)$, except in $S_1 = \#\{x|v_x = 2\} + 3\#\{x|v_x = 3\} + \#\{y|w_y = 2\} + 3\#\{y|w_y = 3\}$ states, where it will contribute nothing to $m(\Gamma)$, and in $S_2 = \#\{x|v_x = 3\} + \#\{y|w_y = 3\}$ states, where it will contribute 1 to $m(\Gamma)$. Thus $m(\Gamma)$ is at least

$$[20 - S_1]/2 + S_2$$

$$= [20 - \#\{x|v_x = 2 \text{ or } v_x = 3\} - \#\{y|w_y = 2 \text{ or } w_y = 3\}]/2.$$

It is easy to see that the minimum is obtained when all v_x and w_y equal 2 and thus $m(\Gamma) \geq 5$.

4.3. *Sequential Debates*

In a sequential debate, one of the debaters, let us say debater 1, is asked to raise an argument and the other debater can respond by raising one argument. In cases where debater 1 raises the argument x, debater 2 raises the argument y, and debater 2 wins the debate, we will say that y counterargues x.

Claim 3. The minimal $m(\Gamma)$ over all sequential debates is three.

Proof.   Consider the sequential debate Γ_1 with the persuasion rule:

If debater 1 argues for	...debater 2 wins if and only if he counterargues with...
1	$\{2\}$
2	$\{3,5\}$
3	$\{4\}$
4	$\{2,5\}$
5	$\{1,4\}$

This debate induces three mistakes, two in favor of debater 1 (in the states (1,1,2,2,2), (2,2,1,1,2)) and one in favor of debater 2 (in state (1,2,1,2,1)). (Note that in this debate, aspect 3, for example, does not counetrargue aspect 1 and aspect 1 does not counterargue aspect 3). We shall now show that for any sequential debate Γ in which debater 1 starts the debate, $m(\Gamma) \geq 3$. Debater 1 has at most five possible moves. After each of these moves, there is a set of counterarguments, which will persuade the listener to select O_2. Thus, there is a set E of at most five sets of aspects, where debater 1 wins the debate at ω if and only if $1(\omega)$ contains one of the sets in E. ☐

Assume that $m(\Gamma) \leq 2$. No $e \in E$ is a singleton since, had there been one, it would have induced, by itself, five mistakes in favor of debater 1. Any $e \in E$ that consists of two aspects induces one mistake. Thus, E can include at most two sets of size 2. Let $\Omega = \{\omega | n_1(\omega) = 3\}$. This set contains ten states.

If no set in E contains two aspects, there is a mistake in each of the five states in Ω for which $1(\omega)$ is not a set in E.

If there is only one set in E that contains exactly two aspects, then there are at most $3 + 4$ states in Ω in which debater 1 can win the induced game (three states in which $1(\omega)$ contains the set of two aspects in E and at most four states in which $n_1(\omega) = 3$ and $1(\omega)$ is an element in E). Thus, there are at least four mistakes (one in favor of debater 1 and three in favor of debater 2).

Suppose that E contains precisely two sets of two elements. There are at most six sets in Ω for which $1(\omega)$ contains one of these sets. Thus, there must be at least one element in Ω for which $1(\omega)$ does not include a set in E and the number of mistakes must be at least 3.

Claim 4. Any optimal persuasion rule violates the DC principle.

Proof.   By the proof of Claim 3, E does not contain any set of size greater than 3 and contains no more than three sets of size 3. Thus, the number of two-element sets, $\{x, y\}$, which are subsets of a set in E, cannot exceed 8 and, hence, there must be two elements, x and y, so that neither x counterargues y nor y counterargues x.   □

5. Comments

5.1. *The Sequential Debate Game*

In the above analysis, the persuasion rule was a part of the design of the mechanism. The listener was not a player in the game. Alternatively, one could think of a sequential debate as a three-stage game in which the listener, after listening to the two arguments, chooses an outcome, with the aim of maximizing the probability that he will choose the correct one. The set of the listener's strategies is the set of all possible persuasion rules for sequential debates.

First, let us check whether the optimal persuasion rules are sequential equilibrium strategies of the extended game. Consider, for example, the persuasion rule described in Claim 3. This persuasion rule is supported by the following sequential equilibrium of the extended game:

- Debater 1's strategy is to raise the first argument, if there is one, for which debater 2 does not have a proper counterargument. Otherwise, debater 1 chooses the first argument which supports him.
- Debater 2's strategy is to respond with the first successful counterargument whenever he has one and, otherwise, to raise the first argument that supports his position.

- The listener chooses the outcome according to the persuasion rule described in the table in the proof of Claim 3.

The full proof that these three strategies indeed constitute a sequential equilibrium consists in dealing with many cases. We make do with demonstrating some of them:

If debater 1 raises argument 1 and debater 2 responds with argument 3, the listener assigns a probability 0.75 that the correct outcome is O_1; if debater 2 responds with 4 or 5, the listener concludes that the correct outcome is O_1 with certainty. If debater 2 responds with argument 2, the listener concludes that aspect 1 is in favor of debater 1 and, in addition to aspect 2, at least one aspect in $\{3, 4\}$ and one aspect in $\{4, 5\}$ are in favor of debater 2; thus the probability that the correct outcome is O_1 is 0.2.

If debater 1 raises argument 2 and debater 2 responds with argument 1 or 4, the listener concludes that 2, 3, and 5 are in favor of 1. On the other hand if debater 2 responds with 3, the listener concludes that aspects 1, 3, and either 4 or 5 are in favor of debater 2. If debater 2 responds with 5, it means that aspect 3 is in favor of debater 1, but 1, 4, and 5 are in favor of debater 2.

The case where debater 1 raises the argument 3 and debater 2 responds with 5 is an "out of equilibrium event." From the fact that debater 1 did not raise argument 1, the listener should conclude that either aspect 1 or aspect 2 is in favor of debater 2, and from the fact that debater 2 responded with 5, the listener should conclude that aspects 1 and 2 are in favor of debater 1. We assign to the listener, at that history, the belief that aspects 1, 2, and 3 are in favor of debater 1.

Note that the three-stage debate game has other sequential equilibria as well. One of them is particularly natural. In any state ω, debater 1 raises the first argument i which is in his favor. Debater 2 responds with the argument j, which is the smallest $j > i$ in his favor, if such an argument exists; otherwise, he responds with the smallest argument which is in his favor. The listener's strategy will be guided by the following logic: Debater 1, in equilibrium, is supposed to raise the first argument in his favor. If he raises argument i, the listener believes that arguments $1, 2, \ldots, i - 1$ are in favor of debater 2. Debater 2, in equilibrium, is supposed to raise the first argument in his favor following argument i. Hence, if debater 2 raises argument j, the listener believes that arguments $i + 1, \ldots, j - 1$ are in favor of debater 1. The listener chooses O_1 if the number of aspects he (the listener) concludes to support 1 is at least the number of those he concludes to support 2. This equilibrium induces seven mistakes.

5.2. Debates Which Are Mixtures between the One Speaker Debate and the Sequential Debate

We restricted the number of arguments which can be raised during a debate to two. This restriction does not preclude another type of debate, a type which was not analyzed in the previous section: Debater 1 makes the first argument and then, depending on which argument was brought up, either debater 1 or debater 2 is required to raise the second argument. One can verify that the minimal $m(\Gamma)$ over these type of debates is also three.

5.3. On the Assumption That a Debater Can Only Raise Arguments

The assumption that the only actions a debater can take are raising arguments is of course restrictive. For example, consider a mechanism where debater 1 is required to list three aspects and debater 2 wins the debate if and only if he shows that one of these aspects has been realized in his favor. This "mistake-free" debate consists of only two moves and requires "proving" only one argument. However, in this paper, we wish to focus on the relationship between arguments and counterarguments and thus we limit the scope of the discussion to debates where a debater can only raise arguments.

Let us also mention that if we retain the assumption that a debater cannot lie, but we allow a debater to raise arguments against himself, there is a mistake-free debate. Consider a debate where, if debater 1 argues that aspect i is in his favor, debater 2 has to counterargue by showing that either aspect $i+1$ (mod 5) or aspect $i+2$ (mod 5) is in his (debater 2's) favor in order to win, and if debater 1 concedes that aspect i is in favor of debater 2, debater 2 has to counterargue by showing that one of the aspects, $i-1$ (mod 5), $i+1$ (mod 5), or $i+2$ (mod 5), is in his (debater 2's) favor in order to win. If $n_1(\omega) \geq 4$, then for some i, the three aspects, i (mod 5), $i+1$ (mod 5), and $i+2$ (mod 5), are in $1(\omega)$; thus, debater 1 can win by raising argument i. If $n_1(\omega) = 3$, then either there is an aspect i so that the three aspects, i (mod 5), $i+1$ (mod 5), and $i+2$ (mod 5) are in $1(\omega)$, and he can win by raising the argument i, or there is an aspect i such that aspects $i-1$ (mod 5), $i+1$ (mod 5), or $i+2$ (mod 5) are in $1(\omega)$, and debater 1 can win by conceding on aspect i. If $n_1(\omega) \leq 2$, debater 2 can rebuff all of debater 1's arguments.

6. Discussion

The reader may wonder why it is that in practice we do not observe persuasion rules of the kind described in Claim 3. Our view is that an important feature of real life persuasion rules is that they are stated in natural language. The persuasion rules we expect to observe are those that are easily definable using a binary relation over the set of aspects, and which the parties naturally associate with the problem. Let us go back to our "five cities" example. The most salient binary relation on the set of these five cities is the one which partitions the set into the "Far East" and the "non-Far East" cities. The sequential debate with the persuasion rule described in Claim 3 cannot be described using these terms alone without referring to the names of the cities. On the other hand, consider the sequential debate with the following persuasion rule: The second speaker is required to counterargue an argument referring to a Far East city with another Far East city and he is required to counterargue a non-Far East city with a non-Far East city. The sequential debate with this persuasion rule induces seven mistakes. This is actually the best persuasion rule from among those which can be described just by using the terms "Far East city" and "non-Far East city" with no references to the names of the cities. Note that the latter sequential debate is worse than the one-speaker debate in which the speaker is required to present two arguments, either from the set of the Far East cities or from the set of the non-Far East cities, in order to win. This one-speaker debate induces only four mistakes.

Our purpose in this paper was not to provide a general theory of debates. The implications of the constraints imposed by the natural language on optimal debates were not studied. Our only purpose was to demonstrate that a phenomenon we often observe in debates can be explained as an outcome of an optimization which takes into account another "real life" constraint: the limit on the amount of information that the listener can process. Thus, during a debate, the relative "strength" of an argument may not derive from the relative "quality" of the information embodied in that argument. Or, put differently, there may be two arguments such that neither is a persuasive counterargument to the other. We show that this phenomenon is not necessarily a rhetorical fallacy; instead it may be consistent with the outcome of a constrained optimization of the debate rules.

We believe that this phenomenon is connected to considerations of pragmatics. Within a debate, a responder counterarguing to "Bangkok" with anything other than Manila is interpreted as an admission that Manila is also an argument in favor of the opponent's position. Or, in the context of question 3, if a debater responds to Tuesday by Thursday, skipping Wednesday, it is considered as an admission that Wednesday does not go in his favor. The fact that the sentence "On Thursday channel B is superior" is uttered as a counterargument to "On Tuesday channel A is superior" gives the sentence a meaning different than what it would have received, had it been stated in isolation.

The fact that, during a conversation, an utterance may acquire meanings beyond those it would have received had it been stated in isolation is related to ideas discussed in the philosophy of language. Grice (1989), in particular, argues that the natural interpretation of utterances in natural language contains more information than the meaning given by the utterances in isolation. We apply an economic approach in the sense that we try to provide a rationale for such phenomena by showing that they are outcomes of the optimization of a certain objective function, subject to constraints (see also Rubinstein, 1996).

7. Related Literature

We find the spirit of Fishman and Hagerty (1990) the closest to ours. The following is one interpretation of their model. A listener wishes to obtain information from one speaker about the state of nature. The state of nature may receive one of two equally likely values, H or L. The speaker observes K signals about the state; each receives the value of the state with probability $p > 1/2$. The speaker aims to increase the probability that the listener assigns to the state H. The constraint on the complexity of the mechanism is that the speaker can present only one signal (he cannot cheat). The "social designer" looks for a persuasion rule that decreases the expected probability that the listener assigns to the false state. The best "persuasion rule" is to order the signals, $s_1, \ldots, s_K$, and to have the listener interpret the signal s_k as an admission by the speaker that the signals $s_1, \ldots, s_{k-1}$ receive the value L. Thus, though all signals are equally informative, the optimal persuasion rule treats them unequally.

Despite its common use in supporting decision-making, little has been said about debates in economics and game theory. Several exceptions are reviewed below.

Austen-Smith (1993) studies cheap talk debates where two parties try to influence the action taken by a third party. Initially, the ideal points of the two players are $+1$ and -1, whereas the third party's ideal point is 0. Each debater gets a signal about a random variable d, which represents for him the shift in his ideal point. The paper investigates the existence of informative equilibria for two types of a cheap talk game, one where the messages are sent simultaneously and the other where the debaters send the messages sequentially. Krishna and Morgan (2001) study a similar game where the experts have full information about a nonbinary state.

Shin (1994) analyzes the sequential equilibria of what he calls a "simultaneous moves game of persuasion" (see also Milgrom and Roberts, 1986). In his work, a state of nature, $x \in \{y_1, \ldots, y_K\}$, is the "true" amount of money that party 2 should pay to party 1. For each k, each of the two parties receives (with some probability) a signal that tells him whether $x < y_k$ or $x \geq y_k$. A party cannot present a wrong signal but *does not have* to disclose all the signals he has received. The two debaters move simultaneously, disclosing whichever signals they decide to reveal to a third party who then determines the amount of money that party 2 will pay party 1. The third party's goal is to decrease the expected distance between his own ruling and the "right" amount (the state). Shin (1994) shows that there is a sequential equilibrium with a simple, attractive structure, according to which each of the two parties reports only good news, namely, signals which confirm that the state is above (or below) a certain cutoff point.

Lipman and Seppi (1995) study another phenomenon, often observed in real life: debaters who convey wrong information are severely punished. They study a model in which a debater can present messages as well as bring evidence to refute an opponent's claims. They argue that "little provability" is sufficient for the existence of an equilibrium in which the listener believes a certain party, unless that party's claim is refuted.

Spector (2000) considers a debate between two parties. Each party tries to "move" the position held by the other party (a point in an Euclidean space) closer to his (the first party's) position. The situation is analyzed as a multi-stage game. At each period, one debater gets information about the true state in the form of a signal and he has to choose whether to disclose the signal to the other debater. If a debater presents evidence, it is evaluated by his opponent by taking into account strategic considerations. The paper shows that the debaters' positions will "converge" to "a stable configuration of positions." in which no evidence presented by one debater can change the position held by the other.

References

Austin-Smith, D. (1993). "Interested Experts and Policy Advice: Multiple Referrals under Open Rule," *Games Econ. Behav.* **5**, 3–43.

Fishman, M. J., and K. H. Hagerty (1990). "The Optimal Amount of Discretion to Allow in Disclosures," *Quart. J. Econ.* **105**, 427–444.

Grice, P. (1989). *Studies in the Way of Words.* Cambridge, MA: Harvard Univ. Press.

Krishna, V., and Morgan, J. (2001). "A Model of Expertise," *Quart. J. Econ.*, in press.

Lipman, B. L., and Seppi, D. J. (1995). "Robust Inference in Communication Games with Partial Provability," *J. Econ. Theory* **66**, 370–405.

Milgrom, P., and Roberts, J. (1986). "Relying on the Information of Interested Parties," *Rand. J. Econ.* **17**, 18–32.

Rubinstein, A. (1996). "Why are Certain Properties of Binary Relations Relatively More Common in Natural Language?" *Econometrica* **64**, 343–356.

Shin, H. S. (1994). "The Burden of Proof in a Game of Persuasion," *J. Econ. Theory* **64**, 253–264.

Spector, D. (2000). "Rational Debate and One-Dimensional Conflict," *Quart. J. Econ.* **115**, 181–200.

Chapter 4

On Optimal Rules of Persuasion*

Jacob Glazer

Faculty of Management, Tel Aviv University
Tel Aviv, Israel 69978

Department of Economics, Boston University
Boston, MA, U.S.A.
glazer@post.tau.ac.il

Ariel Rubinstein[†]

School of Economics, Tel Aviv University
Tel Aviv, Israel 69978

Department of Economics, New York University
New York, NY, U.S.A.
rariel@post.tau.ac.il

A speaker wishes to persuade a listener to accept a certain request. The conditions under which the request is justified, from the listener's point of view, depend on the values of two aspects. The values of the aspects are known only to the speaker and the listener can check the value of at most one. A mechanism specifies a set of messages that the speaker can send and a rule that determines the listener's response, namely, which aspect he checks and whether he accepts or rejects the speaker's request. We study mechanisms that maximize the probability that the listener accepts the request when it is justified and rejects the request when it is unjustified, given that the speaker maximizes the probability that his request is accepted. We show that a simple optimal mechanism exists and can be found by solving a linear programming problem in which the set of constraints is derived from what we call the *L*-principle.

Keywords: Persuasion, mechanism design, hard evidence, debates.

*Before reading the paper we advise you to play our "Persuasion Game" on-line: http://gametheory.tau.ac.il/exp5/.
†We are grateful to Noga Alon of Tel Aviv University for numerous discussions and assistance regarding Proposition 2. We also thank the co-editor of this journal, two anonymous referees, Andrew Caplin, and Bart Lipman for valuable comments.

1. Introduction

Our model deals with the situation in which one agent (*the speaker*) wishes to persuade another agent (*the listener*) to take a certain action. Whether or not the listener should take the action is dependent on information possessed by the speaker. The listener can obtain bits of relevant information but is restricted as to the total amount of evidence he can accumulate. The speaker can use only verbal statements to persuade. Whether or not the listener is persuaded is dependent on both the speaker's arguments and the hard evidence the listener has acquired.

Following are some real life examples:

A worker wishes to be hired by an employer for a certain position. The worker tells the employer about his previous experience in two similar jobs. The employer wishes to hire the worker if his average performance in the two previous jobs was above a certain minimal level. However, before making the final decision the employer has sufficient time to thoroughly interview at most one of the candidate's previous employers.

A suspect is arrested on the basis of testimonies provided by two witnesses. The suspect's lawyer claims that their testimonies to the police have serious inconsistencies and therefore his client should be released. The judge's preferred decision rule is to release the suspect only if the two testimonies substantially contradict one another; however, he is able to investigate at most one of the two witnesses.

A doctor claims that he has correctly used two procedures to treat a patient who suffers from two chronic illnesses. An investigator on the case is asked to determine whether the combination of the two procedures was harmful. The investigator has access to the doctor's full report but verifying the details of more than one procedure would be too costly.

A decision maker asks a consultant for advice on whether or not to take on a particular project. The decision maker knows that the consultant is better informed about the state of the world than he is, but he also knows that it is in the consultant's interests that the project be carried out regardless of the state of the world. The decision maker is able to verify only a restricted number of facts that the consultant claims to be true.

In our model the listener has to choose between two actions a and r. A speaker's type is a realization of two aspects initially known only to the speaker. The listener's preferred action critically depends on the speaker's type whereas the speaker would like the listener to choose the action a regardless of his type.

We study a family of mechanisms in which the speaker sends a message to the listener and the listener can then choose to ascertain the realization of at most one of the two aspects. On the basis of the speaker's message and the acquired "hard" evidence, the listener is either persuaded to take the speaker's favorite action a or not. More specifically, a mechanism is composed of three elements: a set of messages from which the speaker can choose; a function that specifies which aspect is to be checked depending on the speaker's message; and the action the listener finally takes as a function of the message sent by the speaker and the acquired information.

Two types of mechanisms will serve a special role in our analysis:

(A) Deterministic mechanisms — for each of the two aspects certain criteria are determined and the speaker's preferred action is chosen if he can show that his type meets these prespecified criteria in at least one of the two aspects. In the first example above, a deterministic mechanism would be equivalent to asking the worker to provide a reference from one of his two previous employers that meets certain criteria.

(B) Random mechanisms — the speaker is asked to report his type; one aspect is then chosen randomly and checked; and the action a is taken if and only if the speaker's report is not refuted. Returning to the first example above, a random mechanism would involve first asking the worker to justify his application by reporting his performance in each of his previous two jobs. Based on his report, the employer then randomly selects one of the two previous employers to interview and accepts the applicant if his report is not refuted.

We are interested in the properties of the mechanisms that are optimal from the point of view of the listener, namely, those in which it is least likely that the listener will choose the wrong action given that the speaker maximizes the probability that the action a will be taken. In our scenario, the listener does not have tools to deter the speaker from cheating and thus we can expect that the speaker will always argue that his information indicates that the action a should be taken. The problem therefore is to decide which rules the listener should follow in order to minimize the probability of making a mistake.

The main results of the paper are as follows:

(i) An optimal mechanism can be found by solving an auxiliary linear programming problem. The objective in the auxiliary problem is to minimize the probability of a mistake. The constraints are derived from a condition that we call the L-principle, which can be demonstrated using the first example above: Assume that the worker's performances in each job is classified as good or bad and that the employer wishes to hire the worker only if his performance in both previous jobs was good. Consider the worker's three types: his performance was good in two previous jobs, good only in the first job and good only in the second job. The L-principle says that for any mechanism, the sum of the probabilities of a mistake conditional on each of the three worker's types is at least one.

(ii) An optimal mechanism with a very simple structure always exists. First, the speaker is asked to report his type. If the speaker admits that the action r should be taken, then the listener chooses r. If the speaker claims that the action a should be taken, the listener tosses a fair coin where on each of its two sides one of three symbols, r, 1, or 2 appears (the degenerate case where the same symbol appears on both sides is not excluded). The meaning of the symbol r is that the listener chooses the action r. The meaning of the symbol $i = 1$, 2 is that the listener checks aspect i and takes the action a if and only if the speaker's claim regarding this aspect is confirmed.

(iii) The optimal mechanism is credible, that is, there exists an optimal strategy for the speaker that induces beliefs that make it optimal for the listener to follow the mechanism. Furthermore, the speaker's optimal strategy can be derived from the dual (auxiliary) linear programming problem.

(iv) For the case that all types are equally likely, we identify certain "convexity" and "monotonicity" conditions under which there exists an optimal mechanism that is deterministic.

2. The Model

Let $\{1, \ldots, n\}$ be a set of random variables that we call *aspects*. Most of the analysis will be conducted for $n = 2$. The realization of aspect k is a member of a set X_k. A *problem* is (X, A, p), where $\emptyset = A \subset X = \times_{k=1,\ldots,n} X_k$ and p is a probability measure on X. We use the notation p_x for the probability of type x, that is $p_x = p(\{x\})$. For the case that X is infinite we relate to p_x as a density function. For simplicity, we assume that $p_x > 0$ for all x. A problem is *finite* if the set X is finite. There are two agents: the *speaker* and the *listener*. A member of X is called a (speaker's) *type* and is interpreted as a possible characterization of the speaker. The listener has to take one of two actions: a (accept) or r (reject). The listener is interested in taking the action a if the speaker's type is in A and the action r if the type is in $R = X - A$. The speaker, regardless of his type, prefers the listener to take the action a. The speaker knows his type while the listener only knows its distribution. The listener can *check*, that is, find out the realization of, at most one of the n aspects.

A *mechanism* is (M, f), where M is a set (of *messages*) and f: $M \to Q$ where Q is the set of all lotteries $\langle \pi_0, d_0; \pi_1, d_1; \ldots; \pi_n, d_n \rangle$ where $(\pi_i)_{i=0,1,\ldots,n}$ is a probability vector and $d_k \colon X_k \to \{a, r\}$ where $X_0 = \{e\}$ is an arbitrary singleton set (that is, d_0 is a constant). An element in Q is interpreted as a possible response of the listener to a message. With probability π_0 no aspect is checked and the action $d_0 \in \{a, r\}$ is taken, and with probability $\pi_k (k = 1, \ldots, n)$ aspect k is checked and if its realization is x_k the action $d_k(x_k)$ is taken. Our choice of the set Q captures the assumptions that the listener can check at most one aspect and that the aspect to be checked can be selected randomly.

A *direct mechanism* is one where $M = X$. For a direct mechanism (X, f) we say that following a message m the mechanism *verifies aspect k with probability* π_k when $f(m) = (\pi_0, d_0; \pi_1, d_1; \ldots; \pi_n, d_n)$ is such that $d_k(x_k) = a$ iff $x_k = m_k$. The *fair random mechanism* is the direct mechanism according to which, for every $m \in A$, the listener verifies each aspect with probability $1/n$ and, for every $m \in R$, he chooses the action r. A mechanism is *deterministic* if for every $m \in M$ the lottery $f(m)$ is degenerate (that is, for some k, $\pi_k = 1$).

For every lottery $q = \langle \pi_0, d_0; \pi_1, d_1; \ldots; \pi_n, d_n \rangle$ and every type x define $q(x)$ to be the probability that the action a is taken when the lottery q is applied to type x, that is, $q(x) = \sum_{\{k|d_k(x_k)=a\}} \pi_k$. We assume that given a mechanism (M, f) a speaker of type x will choose a message that maximizes the probability that the action a is taken, namely he chooses a message $m \in M$ that maximizes $f(m)(x)$. Let μ_x be the probability that the listener takes the wrong action with respect to type x, assuming the speaker's behavior. That is, for $x \in R$ we have $\mu_x = \max_{m \in M} f(m)(x)$ and for $x \in A$ we have $\mu_x = 1 - \max_{m \in M} f(m)(x)$. Note that all solutions to the speaker's maximization problem induce the same probability of a mistake. We will refer to $(\mu_x)_{x \in X}$ as the vector of mistakes induced by the mechanism. The *mistake probability* induced by the mechanism is $\int_{x \in X} p_x \mu_x$.

The mechanisms are evaluated according to the listener's interests while ignoring those of the speaker. We assume that the listener's loss given a mechanism is the mistake probability induced by the mechanism. Thus, given a problem (X, A, p), an *optimal mechanism* is one that minimizes the mistake probability. None of our results will change if we modify the listeners's loss to $\int_{x \in X} p_x c_x \mu_x$ where c_x is interpreted as the listener's cost from taking the wrong action when the speaker's type is x.

It should be mentioned that we do not restrict the discussion to direct mechanisms and do not apply the revelation principle.

Following is a concrete example:

Example 1. Let $A_1 = A_2 = [0, 1]$, let $A = \{(x_1, x_2) | x_1 + x_2 \geq 1\}$, and let p be the uniform distribution.

If the listener chooses to ignore the speaker's message, the lowest probability of a mistake he can obtain is $1/4$. This mistake probability can be achieved by a mechanism in which aspect 1 is checked with probability 1 and action a is taken iff aspect 1's value is at least $1/2$ (formally, $M = \{e\}$ and $f(e)$ is the degenerate lottery where $\pi_1 = 1$ and $d_1(x_1) = a$ iff $x_1 \geq 1/2$).

In this example, letting the speaker talk can improve matters. Consider the following deterministic direct mechanism $(M = X)$ characterized by two numbers z_1 and z_2. Following the receipt of a message (m_1, m_2), the speaker verifies the value of aspect 1 if $m_1 \geq z_1$ and verifies the value of aspect 2 if $m_1 < z_1$ but $m_2 \geq z_2$. If $m_k < z_k$ for both k the action r is taken. One interpretation of this mechanism is that in order to persuade the listener, the speaker has to show that the realization of at least one of the aspects is above some threshold (which may be different for each aspect). The set of types for which the listener's action will be wrong consists of the three shaded triangles shown in Figure 1a.

One can see that the optimal thresholds are $z_1 = z_2 = 2/3$ yielding a mistake probability of $1/6$. Is it possible to obtain a lower probability of a mistake by applying a nondeterministic mechanism? (Notice that the fair random mechanism does not help here as it yields mistake probability of $1/4$.) We will return to this question later.

3. A Basic Proposition

From now on, assume $n = 2$. For simplicity of notation, we write μ_{ij} for $\mu_{(i,j)}$. The following proposition is key to our analysis (note that it is valid

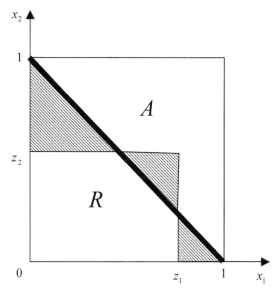

Figure 1a.

for both finite and infinite X and for any p):

Proposition 0. (The L-Principle) *Let (X, A, p) be a problem. For any mechanism and for any three types $(i, j) \in A$, $(i, s) \in R$, and $(t, j) \in R$, it must be that $\mu_{ij} + \mu_{is} + \mu_{tj} \geq 1$.*

Proof. Let (M, f) be a mechanism. Let m be a message optimal for type (i, j) and let $f(m) = (\pi_0, d_0; \pi_1, d_1; \pi_2, d_2)$. For a proposition e, let δ_e be 1 if e is true and 0 if e is false. Then

$$\mu_{ij} = \pi_0 \delta_{d_0 = r} + \pi_1 \delta_{d_1(i) = r} + \pi_2 \delta_{d_2(j) = r}.$$

If type (i, s) sends the message m ("claims" that he is (i, j)) the action a will be taken with probability $\pi_0 \delta_{d_0 = a} + \pi_1 \delta_{d_1(i) = a}$ and therefore

$$\mu_{is} \geq \pi_0 \delta_{d_0 = a} + \pi_1 \delta_{d_1(i) = a}.$$

Similarly,

$$\mu_{ij} \geq \pi_0 \delta_{d_0 = a} + \pi_2 \delta_{d_2(j) = a}.$$

Therefore

$$\mu_{ij} + \mu_{is} + \mu_{tj} \geq \pi_0 \delta_{d_0=r} + \pi_1 \delta_{d_1(i)=r} + \pi_2 \delta_{d_2(j)=r}$$
$$+ \pi_0 \delta_{d_0=a} + \pi_1 \delta_{d_1(i)=a} + \pi_0 \delta_{d_0=a} + \pi_2 \delta_{d_2(j)=a}$$
$$= 1 + \pi_0 \delta_{d_0=a} \geq 1. \qquad \Box$$

The idea of the proof is as follows: whatever is the outcome of the randomization following a message m sent by type $(i,j) \in A$, either the mistaken action r is taken, or at least one of the two types (i,s) and (t,j) in R can induce the wrong action a by sending m.

We define an L to be any set of three types $(i,j) \in A$, $(i,s) \in R$, and $(t,j) \in R$. We refer to the result of Proposition 0 (the sum of mistakes in every L is at least 1) as the L-principle. Extending the L-principle to the case of $n > 2$ is done by defining an L to be a set of three types $x \in A$, $y \in R$, and $z \in R$ such that y and z each differs from x in the value of exactly one aspect.

4. Examples

In all our examples we take p to be uniform. For the case that X is finite we will refer to $\sum_{x \in X} \mu_x$ as the *number of mistakes*. When p is uniform and X is finite, an optimal mechanism can be found by using a technique that relies on the L-principle: finding a mechanism that induces H mistakes and finding H disjoint L's allows us to conclude that this mechanism is optimal, thus yielding a mistake probability of $H/|X|$. The examples also give some intuition as to when optimality can be obtained by deterministic mechanisms and when it requires that the listener use randomization to determine the aspect to be checked.

Example 2. Let $X_1 = X_2 = \{1, \ldots, 5\}$ and $A = \{x | x_1 + x_2 \geq 7\}$. In Figure 2, each entry stands for an element in X and the types in A are

1	A 1	A	A	A
2	5	A 2	A 5	A
3			A 3	A
4			5	A 4
	1	2	3	4

Figure 2.

indicated by the letter A. We mark 5 *disjoint* L's (the three elements of each L are indicated by the same number).

Following is a direct mechanism that induces 5 mistakes and is thus optimal: For any message m such that $m_k \leq 4$ for both k, the action r is taken. Otherwise, an aspect k, for which $m_k = 5$, is verified. In fact, this mechanism amounts to simply asking the speaker to present an aspect with a value of 5. The five mistakes are with respect to the three types (3,4), (4,4), and (4,3) in A and the two types (1, 5) and (5,1) in R.

Example 2 later will be generalized: when p is uniform, constructing an optimal mechanism does not require randomization when the speaker's aim is to persuade the listener that the average of the values of the two aspects is above a certain threshold.

Example 3. This example shows that the the conclusion of Example 2 (randomization is not needed for the case in which the speaker tries to persuade the listener that the average of the values of the two aspects is above a certain threshold) does not hold for the case in which the number of aspects is greater than 2.

Consider the problem where $n = 3$, $X_k = \{0, 1\}$ for $k = 1, 2, 3$, and $A = \{(x_1, x_2, x_3) | \sum_k x_k \geq 2\}$. Consider the mechanism where the speaker is asked to name two aspects, the listener checks each of them with probability $1/2$ and takes the action a if the value of the checked aspect is 1. This mechanism yields 1.5 mistakes (mistake probability of $3/16$ since only the three types (1,0,0), (0,1,0), and (0,0,1) can each mislead the listener with probability $1/2$.

To see that this is an optimal mechanism note that the following three inequalities hold:

$$\mu_{(1,1,0)} + \mu_{(1,0,0)} + \mu_{(0,1,0)} \geq 1,$$
$$\mu_{(1,0,1)} + \mu_{(1,0,0)} + \mu_{(0,0,1)} \geq 1,$$
$$\mu_{(0,1,1)} + \mu_{(0,1,0)} + \mu_{(0,0,1)} \geq 1.$$

The minimum of $\sum_{x \in X} \mu_x$ subject to the constraint

$$\sum_{\{x | x_1 + x_2 + x_3 = 2\}} \mu_x + 2 \sum_{\{x | x_1 + x_2 + x_3 = 1\}} \mu_x \geq 3,$$

implied by summing up the three inequalities, is attained when $\mu_x = 1/2$ for any $x \in \{(1, 0, 0), (0, 1, 0), (0, 0, 1)\}$ and $\mu_x = 0$ for any other $x \in X$. Thus, the number of mistakes cannot fall below 1.5.

The number of mistakes induced by a determinstic mechanism must be an integer and thus, for this problem, it is at least 2. One optimal mechanism within the set of deterministic mechanisms involves taking the action a iff the speaker can show that either aspect 1 or aspect 2 has the value 1. This mechanism induces two mistakes with regard to types $(1, 0, 0)$ and $(0,1, 0)$.

Example 4. This corresponds to the situation described in the Introduction in which a suspect's lawyer claims that the two testimonies brought against his client are inconsistent but the judge has time to thoroughly investigate only one of them. Consider the problem where $X_1 = X_2 = \{1, 2, 3, \ldots, I\}$ and $A = \{(x_1, x_2)|x_1 \neq x_2\}$. Intuitively, the knowledge of the value of only one aspect by itself is not useful to the listener. The optimal mechanism will be shown to be nondeterministic in this case.

The fair random mechanism (following a message in A each of the two aspects is verified with probability .5) induces $I/2$ mistakes. The minimal number of mistakes is $I/2$. The two cases $I = 2$ and $I = 3$ are illustrated in Figures 3a and 3b.

In the case of $I = 2$ there is one L. For $I = 3$, the maximal number of disjoint L's is one; however, notice the six starred types — three in A and three in R. Each of the starred types in A combined with two of the starred types in R constitutes an L. Therefore, any mechanism induces mistake probabilities $(\mu_x)_{x \in X}$ satisfying:

$$\mu_{1,3} + \mu_{1,1} + \mu_{3,3} \geq 1,$$
$$\mu_{1,2} + \mu_{1,1} + \mu_{2,2} \geq 1,$$
$$\mu_{2,3} + \mu_{2,2} + \mu_{3,3} \geq 1,$$

which imply that the sum of mistakes with respect to these six elements must be at least 1.5. The generalization for $I > 3$ is obvious.

Any deterministic mechanism induces a vector $(\mu_x)_{x \in X}$ of mistakes with $\mu_x \in \{0, 1\}$ for all x. If there is an i for which $\mu_{ii} = 0$, then for any $j \neq i$ either $\mu_{jj} = 1$ or $\mu_{i,j} = 1$ since if $\mu_{jj} = 0$ the constraint

1	$R\,1$
$R\,1$	

(a)

$*$	$*$	$R\,*$
$*$	$R\,*$	
$R\,*$		

(b)

Figure 3.

$\mu_{i,j} + \mu_{ii} + \mu_{j,j} \geq 1$ implies $\mu_{i,j} = 1$. Therefore $\sum_{x \in X} \mu_x \geq I - 1$. Thus, any deterministic mechanism induces at least $I - 1$ mistakes.

A deterministic mechanism that induces $I - 1$ mistakes is the one in which the speaker is asked to present an aspect whose realization is not 1 (thus yielding mistakes only for the types (i, i) with $i \neq 1$).

Example 5. Whereas in Example 4 the speaker tries to persuade the listener that the two aspects have different values, here he tries to persuade him that they have the same value. That is, $X_1 = X_2 = \{1, \ldots, I\}$ and $A = \{x | (x_1, x_2) | x_1 = x_2\}$. Here, it is also true that any information about one of the aspects provides no useful information to the listener but unlike the previous case, for $I \geq 2$, randomization is not helpful. The mechanism according to which the listener chooses r independently of the speaker's message without checking any of the aspects induces I mistakes. To see that one cannot reduce the number of mistakes note that the I sets $\{(i, i), (i + 1, i), (i, i + 1)\}$ for $i = 1, \ldots, I - 1$ and $\{(I, I), (1, I), (I, 1)\}$ consist of a collection of disjoint L's.

Comment. In Example 5 with $I = 3$ the probability of a mistake is $1/3$. This is in fact the worst case for the listener, that is the optimal mechanism in our model with two aspects and any probability measure will never induce a mistake probability that is higher than $1/3$. Actually, in every problem, either the "reject all" mechanism or the fair random mechanism guarantees a mistake probability of at most $1/3$. If the probability of the set A is δ, then the "reject all" mechanism yields mistake probabilities of δ, the fair random mechanism yields the mistake probability of at most $(1 - \delta)/2$ and $\min\{\delta, (1 - \delta)/2\} \leq 1/3$.

Example 6. As mentioned above, the optimality criterion we employ involves maximizing the probability that the listener makes the right decision from his point of view while ignoring the interests of the speaker. If the optimality criterion also took into account the speaker's interests, the optimal mechanism would of course change. In particular, as this example shows, the listener might be indifferent between two optimal mechanisms while the speaker might not.

Consider the problem with $X = \{1, \ldots, 5\} \times \{1, \ldots, 5\}$ and $A = \{(x_1, x_2) | x_1 + x_2 \in \{6, 8, 10\}\}$. The minimal number of mistakes is easily shown to be 8 and is obtained by both the deterministic mechanism "show me an aspect whose value is 5" and the fair random mechanism. However, under the fair random mechanism the listener can induce the action a with

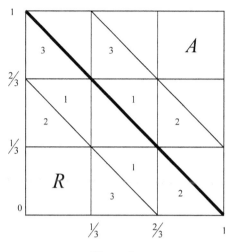

Figure 1b.

probability $17/25$ whereas under the optimal deterministic mechanism he can do so only with probability $9/25$. Thus, the fair random mechanism is superior for the speaker.

Let us return to Example 1 and demonstrate the usefulness of the L-principle also in cases where the problem is not finite.

Example 1. (Continued). We have already found a deterministic mechanism with mistake probability of $1/6$. To see that the mistake probability of any mechanism is at least $1/6$, divide the unit square into 9 equal squares and divide each square into two triangles as shown in Figure 1b.

The set $T_1 = \{(x_1, x_2) \in A | x_1 \leq 2/3 \text{ and } x_2 \leq 2/3\}$ is one of the three triangles denoted in the figure by the number 1. Any three points $x = (x_1, x_2) \in T_1, y = (x_1 - 1/3, x_2) \in R$, and $z = (x_1, x_2 - 1/3) \in R$ establish an L. By Proposition 0, $\mu_x + \mu_y + \mu_z \geq 1$. The collection of all these L's is a set of disjoint sets whose union is the three triangles denoted in the figure by the number 1. Therefore the integral of μ over these three triangles must be at least the size of T_1, namely $1/18$. Similar considerations regarding the three triangles denoted by the number 2 and the three triangles denoted by the number 3 imply that $\int_{x \in X} \mu_x \geq 1/6$.

5. An Equivalent Linear Programming Problem

We will now show that for a finite problem, finding an optimal mechanism is equivalent to solving an auxiliary linear programming problem.

Let (X, A, p) be a finite problem. Define $P(X, A, p)$ to be the linear programming problem:

$$\min \sum_{x \in X} p_x \kappa_x \text{ subject to}$$

$$\kappa_{ij} + \kappa_{is} + \kappa_{ij} \geq 1 \quad \text{for all } (i, j) \in A, \ (i, s) \in R, \quad \text{and} \quad (t, j) \in R, \quad \text{and}$$

$$0 \leq \kappa_x \quad \text{for all } x \in X.$$

We will show that the solution to $P(X, A, p)$ coincides with the vector of mistake probabilities induced by an optimal mechanism.

Note that not every vector that satisfies the constraints of $P(X, A, p)$, even if we add the constraints $\kappa_x \leq 1$ for all x, can be induced by a mechanism. "Incentive compatibility" implies additional constraints on the vector of mistake probabilities, $(\mu_x)_{x \in X}$, induced by a mechanism. For example, if $(i, j) \in A$, $(i, s) \in A$, and $(t, j) \in A$, then it is impossible that $\mu_{ij} = 0$ while both $\mu_{is} = 1$ and $\mu_{tj} = 1$, since at least one of the types, (i, s) or (t, j), can increase the probability that the action taken is a by imitating type (i, j). Nevertheless, we will show that any solution to the linear programming problem can be induced by a mechanism.

Proposition 1. *Let (X, A, p) be a finite problem and let $(\kappa_x)_{x \in X}$ be a solution to $P(X, A, p)$. Then, there is an optimal mechanism such that the vector of mistakes induced by the mechanism is $(\kappa_x)_{x \in X}$.*

Proof.
Step 1: Note that for every $x \in X$ it must be that $\kappa_x \leq 1$ and either $\kappa_x = 0$ or there are two other types y and z such that $\{x, y, z\}$ establish an L and $\kappa_x + \kappa_y + \kappa_z = 1$. Otherwise we could reduce κ_x and stay within the constraints.

Step 2: By Proposition 0 any vector of mistake probabilities induced by a mechanism satisfies the constraints. Thus, it is sufficient to construct a mechanism such that $(\mu_x)_{x \in X}$, the vector of its induced mistake probabilities, is equal to $(\kappa_x)_{x \in X}$.

Choose $M = X$. We use the convention $\min_{x \in \emptyset} \kappa_x = 1$. For any message in R the action r is chosen.

For a message $(i, j) \in A$, distinguish between two cases:

(i) $\kappa_{ij} \geq 0$:

- with probability κ_{ij} the action r is taken.
- with probability $\min_{\{s|is \in R\}} \kappa_{is}$ the first aspect is verified.
- with probability $\min_{\{t|tj \in R\}} \kappa_{ij}$ the second aspect is verified.

By Step 1, $\kappa_{ij} + \min_{\{s|is \in R\}} \kappa_{is} + \min_{\{t|tj \in R\}} \kappa_{tj} = 1$.

(ii) $\kappa_{ij} = 0$: Note that $\min_{\{s|is \in R\}} \kappa_{is} + \min_{\{t|tj \in R\}} \kappa_{tj} \geq 1$. Choose two numbers $\alpha_1 \leq \min_{\{s|is \in R\}} \kappa_{is}$ and $\alpha_2 \leq \min_{\{t|tj \in R\}} \kappa_{tj}$ satisfying $\alpha_1 + \alpha_2 = 1$. Aspect 1 (2) is verified with probability $\alpha_1(\alpha_2)$.

Step 3: We will now show that for the mechanism constructed in Step 2, $\mu_x \leq \kappa_x$ for every $x \in X$.

A type $(i, j) \in R$ cannot induce the action a with positive probability unless he sends a message $(i, s^*) \in A$ or $(t^*, j) \in A$. If he announces (i, s^*) the first aspect is verified with probability of at most $\min_{\{s|is \in R\}} \kappa_{is} \leq \kappa_{ij}$. If he sends the message (t^*, j) the second aspect is verified with probability of at most $\min_{\{t|tj \in R\}} \kappa_{tj} \leq \kappa_{ij}$. Thus, (i, j) cannot induce the action a with probability higher than κ_{ij}.

A type $(i, j) \in A$ who announces (i, j) will induce the action a with probability $1 - \kappa_{ij}$. Since his aim is to reduce the probability of a mistake, he will not induce a probability of a mistake higher than κ_{ij}.

Step 4: By Proposition 0, the vector $(\mu_x)_{x \in X}$ satisfies the constraints of $P(X, A, p)$ and by Step 3, the objective function assigns to this vector a value of at most $\sum_{x \in X} p_x \kappa_x$, which is the value of the solution to $P(X, A, p)$. Therefore it must be that $\mu_x = \kappa_x$ for all $x \in X$ and the mechanism we constructed in Step 2 is optimal.   □

6. The Simple Structure of Optimal Mechanisms

Next we will show that there always exists an optimal mechanism with a simple structure. In Step 2 of the proof of Proposition 1 we constructed a direct optimal mechanism in which the listener only verifies aspects. Thus, the fact that we allow the listener to condition his action on the exact value of the aspect he has checked does not enable him to reduce the mistake probability beyond what he could obtain were he only able to *verify* one aspect of the speaker's claim about his type. Proposition 1 by itself does not tell us anything about the probabilities used in an optimal mechanism.

We will now show that for $n = 2$ one can always construct an optimal mechanism using only a fair coin as a form of randomization.

Proposition 2. *For every finite problem (X, A, p) there exists an optimal mechanism that is direct (i.e. $M = X$) such that:*

(a) *If $m \in R$ the listener takes the action r whereas if $m \in A$ the listener does one of the following:*

   (i) *takes the action r;*

   (ii) *takes the action r with probability $1/2$ and verifies one aspect with probability $1/2$;*

   (iii) *verifies each aspect with probability $1/2$;*

   (iv) *verifies one aspect with probability 1.*

   (Using our notation, for every $m \in R$, $f(m)$ is the degenerate lottery r and for every message $m = (m_1, m_2) \in A$, $f(m)$ is a lottery $\langle \pi_0, d_0; \pi_1, d_1; \pi_2, d_2 \rangle$ where all π_i are in $\{0, 1/2, 1\}$, $d_0 = r$, and $d_i(x_i) = a$ iff $x_i = m_i$.)

(b) *It is optimal for type $x \in A$ to report x and for type $x \in R$ to send a message y such that for one aspect k, $x_k = y_k$.*

Proof.   (a) A proposition due to Alon (2003) states that if $(\alpha_x)_{x \in X}$ is an extreme point of the set of all vectors satisfying the constraints in $P(X, A, p)$, then $\alpha_x \in \{0, 1/2, 1\}$ for all $x \in X$. (Actually, our initial conjecture was that $\alpha_x \in \{0, 1\}$ for all $x \in A$ and $\alpha_x \in \{0, 1/2, 1\}$ for all $x \in R$. Alon showed that we were only partially right and proved the modification of our conjecture.)

Let $(\kappa_x)_{x \in X}$ be a solution to $P(X, A, p)$. As a solution to a linear programming problem the vector $(\kappa_x)_{x \in X}$ is an extreme point and thus $\kappa_x \in \{0, 1/2, 1\}$ for all $x \in X$. The construction of an optimal mechanism in Proposition 1 implies the rest of our claim since for every $i \in X_1$ and $j \in X_2$ the numbers $\min_{\{s|is \in R\}} \kappa_{is}$ and $\min_{\{t|tj \in R\}} \kappa_{tj}$ are all within $\{0, 1/2, 1\}$.

(b) The claim is straightforward for $x \in R$ and for $x \in A$ for which $\kappa_x = 0$. Type $(i, j) \in A$ for whom $\kappa_{ij} > 0$ can possibly obtain a positive probability of acceptance only by "cheating" about at most one aspect. If he claims to be type (t, j), then the probability that the second aspect will be verified is at most $\min_{\{t|tj \in R\}} \kappa_{tj}$, which is exactly the probability that aspect 2 is verified when the speaker admits he is (i, j).   □

Example 7.   In all previous examples the mistake probability of a type in A induced by the optimal mechanisms we have constructed was either 0 or 1. In this example any optimal mechanism induces a mistake probability of 0.5 for at least one type in A.

Let $X_1 = \{1, \ldots, 8\}$, $X_2 = \{1, \ldots, 7\}$; the types in A are denoted by A and p is uniform.

Any mechanism for this problem induces at least 16 mistakes since we can find 16 disjoint L's (see Figure 4b where each L is indicated by a distinct number). This number is at most 16 since the vector $\kappa_x = 1/2$ for any of the 32 types indicated by a star in Figure 4a and $\kappa_x = 0$ otherwise, satisfies the constraints of $P(X, A, p)$. Note that $\kappa_{66} = \kappa_{67} = 1/2$ although $(6, 6)$ and $(6, 7)$ are in A.

We will now show that for any $(\kappa_x)_{x \in X}$, a solution for $P(X, A, p)$, either κ_{66} or κ_{67}, is not an integer.

First, note that $\kappa_{66} + \kappa_{67} \leq 1$. In Figure 4c we indicate 15 disjoint L's that do not contain any of the elements in the box $\{6, 7, 8\} \times \{6, 7\}$ and thus the sum of mistakes in that box cannot exceed 1.

The 16 L's in Figure 4b do not contain $(8, 6)$ and $(8, 7)$ and thus $\kappa_{86} = \kappa_{87} = 0$. Similarly, $\kappa_{76} = \kappa_{77} = 0$.

Now assume that both κ_{66} and κ_{67} are integers. Then there is $j \in \{6, 7\}$ so that $\kappa_{6j} = 0$. For any $i = 1, \ldots, 5$ it must be $\kappa_{6j} + \kappa_{6i} + \kappa_{7j} \geq 1$ and thus $\kappa_{6,i} = 1$. However, none of the 12 disjoint L's in Figure 4d contain any of the 5 types $(6, i)$, where $i = 1, \ldots, 5$ and hence the total number of mistakes is at least 17, which is a contradiction!

7. The Listener's Credibility and the Dual Problem

In the construction of the optimal mechanism we have assumed that the listener is committed to the mechanism. It is possible, however, that the listener will calculate the optimal strategy of the speaker given the mechanism and will make an inference from the speaker's message about his type that will lead the listener to prefer not to follow the mechanism.

In other words, one may think about the situation as an extensive game: the speaker first sends a message to the listener; following the message the listener *chooses* which aspect to check and once he has observed the realization of the aspect, he *decides* whether to take the action a or r. A mechanism can be thought of as a listener's strategy in this extensive game. One may ask whether the listener's strategy, which corresponds to an optimal mechanism, is part of a sequential equilibrium for this extensive game. If it is, we will say that the mechanism is *credible*.

*	*	*	*	*	A *		
*	*	*	*	*	A *		
*	A	A	A	A	*	*	*
A	*	A	A	A	*	*	*
A	A	*	A	A	*	*	*
A	A	A	*	A	*	*	*
A	A	A	A	*	*	*	*

(a)

9	10	1	2	5	15A	15	
8	6	3	4	7	16A	16	
11	A	1A	2A	14A	14	1	2
11A	11	3A	4A	A	15	3	4
A	6A	13	12A	5A	12	5	6
8A	A	13A	12	7A	13	7	8
9A	10A	A	A	14	16	9	10

(b)

9	10	1	2	5	A		
8	6	3	4	7	A		
13	11A	1A	2A	A	11	1	2
A	11	3A	4A	12A	12	3	4
13A	6A	14	A	5A	13	5	6
8A	A	14A	15	7A	14	7	8
9A	10A	A	15A	12	15	9	10

(c)

9	10	1	2	5	A		
8	6	3	4	7	A		
11	11A	1A	2A	A		1	2
A	11	3A	4A	A		3	4
A	6A	12	12A	5A		5	6
8A	A	A	12	7A		7	8
9A	10A	A	A			9	10

(d)

Figure 4.

We do not think that the sequential optimality of the listener's mechanism is a crucial criterion for its plausibility. The listener's commitment to the mechanism may arise from considerations external to the model (such as the desire to maintain his reputation). Note also that in our model sequential equilibrium does not impose any restrictions on the beliefs following messages outside the support of the speaker's strategy. This fact makes sequential rationality a rather weak restriction on the listener's strategy.

Nevertheless, the study of the "sequential rationality" of the listener's mechanism yields a surprising result. As we will now see, a solution to the dual linear programming problem of the primal problem studied in Proposition 1 can be transformed into a strategy for the speaker that, together with the listener's strategy as derived in Proposition 1, yield a sequential equilibrium.

The Dual Problem 1. Let (X, A, p) be a problem and let $T(X, A)$ be the set of all its L's. The dual problem to $P(X, A)$ is $D(X, A, p)$:

$$\max \sum_{\Delta \in T(X,A)} \lambda_\Delta \quad \text{subject to}$$

$$\sum_{\{\Delta \in T(X,A) | x \in \Delta\}} \lambda_\Delta \leq p_x \quad \text{for all } x \in X, \quad \text{and}$$

$$0 \leq \lambda_\Delta \quad \text{for all } \Delta \in T(X, A).$$

Recall the examples in Section 4 where $p_x = 1/|X|$ for all $x \in X$. In the analysis of some of these examples we found a number of disjoint L's equal to the number of mistakes induced by some mechanism. Finding a collection of disjoint L's is equivalent to finding a point within the constraints of $D(X, A, p)$ (for which $\lambda_\Delta = 1/|X|$ for any Δ in the collection and $\lambda_\Delta = 0$ for Δ not in the collection). Finding a vector of mistake probabilities induced by a mechanism is equivalent to finding a point within the constraints of $P(X, A, p)$. Thus, our technique is equivalent to the technique commonly used in solving a linear programming problem based on the fact that the values of the solutions of $P(X, A, p)$ and $D(X, A, p)$ coincide.

The analysis of the case in which $I = 3$ in Example 4 can also be viewed in these terms. Assigning $\lambda_\Delta = 1/18$ for the three L's $\{(1, 3), (1, 1), (3, 3)\}$, $\{(1, 2), (1, 1), (2, 2)\}$, and $\{(2, 3), (2, 2), (3, 3)\}$, and $\lambda_\Delta = 0$ otherwise, we identify a point in the constraints of the dual problem with an objective function's value of $1/6$. The fair random mechanism induces the mistake probabilities of $\mu_x = 1/2$ for the three points on the main diagonal and

$\mu_x = 0$ otherwise, yielding the value $1/6$ for the objective function of the primal problem.

Proposition 3. *Let (X, A, p) be a finite problem. An optimal mechanism, built in Propositions 1 and 2 from a solution $(\kappa_x)_{x \in X}$ to $P(X, A, p)$ satisfying that $(\kappa_x)_{x \in X} \in \{0, 1/2, 1\}$ for all $x \in X$, is credible.*

Proof. By the Complementary Slackness Theorem the dual problem $D(X, A, p)$ has a solution $(\lambda_\Delta)_{\Delta \in T(X, A)}$ such that $\lambda_\Delta (1 - \sum_{x \in \Delta} \kappa_x) = 0$ for all $\Delta \in T(X, A)$ and $\kappa_x (p_x - \sum_{x \in \Delta \in T(X, A)} \lambda_\Delta) = 0$ for all $x \in X$. The solutions to the primal and dual problems have the same value, that is, $\sum_{\Delta \in T(X, A)} \lambda_\Delta = \sum_{x \in X} p_x \kappa_x$.

Consider the following speaker's strategy: Let x be a speaker's type. Every $x \in A$ announces x with certainty. Every $x \in R$ announces x with probability $1 - \sum_{\{\Delta \in T(X,A) | x \in \Delta\}} \lambda_\Delta / p_x$ and every Δ with $x \in \Delta$, x announces the unique $y \in A \cap \Delta$ with probability λ_Δ / p_x. This strategy is well defined since by the dual problem constraints $\sum_{\{\Delta \in T(X,A) | x \in \Delta\}} \lambda_\Delta \leq p_x$.

We first show that this strategy is a speaker's best response to the listener's strategy. By Proposition 2 we know that it is optimal for every $x \in A$ to announce x. Let $x \in R$. If $\kappa_x = 0$, type x cannot induce the listener to choose a with a positive probability and any strategy for type x is thus optimal. If $\kappa_x > 0$, then $\sum_{\{\Delta \in T(X,A) | x \in \Delta\}} \lambda_\Delta = p_x$. If a message $z \in A$ is sent by x with a positive probability, then there exists an L, $\Delta = \{z \in A, x \in R, y \in R\}$ for which $\lambda_\Delta > 0$ and thus $\kappa_z + \kappa_x + \kappa_y = 1$. Following are three configurations to consider:

(i) $\kappa_z = 0$, $\kappa_x = \kappa_y = 1/2$.
   After receiving the message z the listener verifies each of the aspects with probability $1/2$. Thus, by sending the message z, type x will induce a with probability $1/2$, which is the best he can do.

(ii) $\kappa_z = 1/2$, $\kappa_x = 1/2$, and $\kappa_y = 0$.
   The listener takes the action r with probability $1/2$ and verifies with probability $1/2$ the aspect k for which $z_k = x_k$. By announcing z, type x induces the action a with probability $1/2$, which is the best he can do.

(iii) $\kappa_z = 0$, $\kappa_x = 1$, and $\kappa_y = 0$.
   The listener verifies with certainty the aspect k for which $z_k = x_k$. Thus, by announcing z type x induces a with probability 1.

It remains to show that this strategy rationalizes the listener's strategy.

Assume $m \in R$ is sent. There is no case in which a message $m \in R$ is sent by a type in A and thus we can assign to the listener the belief that it was sent by a type in R and therefore choosing r is indeed optimal.

Assume $m \in A$ is sent. We distinguish between two cases:

(a) $\kappa_m > 0$: It must be that $\sum_{m \in \Delta \in T(X,A)} \lambda_\Delta = p_m$. The induced Bayesian beliefs assign probability $1/3$ to each of the following three events: the speaker is $m \in A$, the speaker is a type in R that shares with m the value of the first aspect, and the speaker is a type in R that shares with m the value of the second aspect. Conditional on these beliefs, the listener is indifferent between verifying one of the aspects and choosing r, each of which induces a mistake probability of $1/3$.

(b) $\kappa_m = 0$: The induced Bayesian beliefs assign equal probabilities to the event that the speaker is a type $x \in R$ and $x_1 = m_1$ and to the event that the speaker is a type $x \in R$ and $x_2 = m_2$. This probability is not higher than the probability the listener assigns to the event that the speaker is of type m. Thus, verifying any one of the aspects is optimal. □

8. The Optimality of Deterministic Mechanisms

One can think about a deterministic mechanism in the following way: once the speaker has sent the message m, the listener checks one aspect $k(m)$ with probability 1 and chooses a if and only if the value of the aspect is in some set $V(m) \subset X_{k(m)}$. A speaker of type (x_1, x_2) will be able to induce the listener to take the action a if and only if there is a message m such that $x_{k(m)} \in V(m)$. Denote $V_k = \bigcup_{k(m)=k} V(m)$. A type (x_1, x_2) will induce a if and only if $x_k \in V_k$ for at least one k. Thus, for any deterministic mechanism there are two sets $V_1 \subseteq X_1$ and $V_2 \subseteq X_2$ such that the probability of a mistake is the probability of $\{(x_1, x_2) \in A|$ for no $k, x_k \in V_k\} \cup \{(x_1, x_2) \in R|$ for at least one $k, x_k \in V_k\}$. We call V_1 and V_2 the *sets of persuasive facts*.

We now derive a simple necessary condition for a mechanism to be optimal within the set of deterministic mechanisms:

Proposition 4. *Let (X, A, p) be a finite problem. For a mechanism to be optimal within the set of deterministic mechanisms, its sets of persuasive facts V_1 and V_2 must satisfy:*

$$\text{for any } x_1 \in V_1, \quad p\{(x_1, x_2) \in A | x_2 \notin V_2\} \geq p\{(x_1, x_2) \in R | x_2 \notin V_2\}$$

and

for any $x_1 \notin V_1,$ $p\{(x_1, x_2) \in A | x_2 \notin V_2\} \leq p\{(x_1, x_2) \in R | x_2 \notin V_2\}.$

Similar conditions hold for V_2.

Proof.   Assume, for example, that $s \in V_1$ but that

$$p\{(s, X_2) \in A | x_2 \notin V_2\} < p\{(s, x_2) \in R | x_2 \notin V_2\}.$$

Eliminating s from V_1 will decrease the mistake probability. To see this, note first that every type x such that either $x_1 \neq s$ or $x_2 \in V_2$ can induce the action a iff he could induce it prior to the elimination of s from V_1. Any type x such that $x_1 = s$ and $x_2 \notin V_2$ could induce the action a prior to the elimination but cannot do so following it. Thus, elimination of such an s reduces the mistake probability.   □

The condition stated in Proposition 4 is necessary but not sufficient for a mechanism to be optimal within the set of deterministic mechanisms: Returning to Example 4 with $X_1 = X_2 = \{1, 2, 3, 4\}$, a mechanism with $V_1 = V_2 = \{3, 4\}$ satisfies the conditions in the proposition and yields 4 mistakes, while the mechanism with $V_1 = V_2 = \{2, 3, 4\}$ yields only 3 mistakes.

Finally, for problems with uniform probability we will identify conditions that guarantee that there exists an optimal mechanism which is deterministic. Let $X \subseteq \Re^2$. We say that a set $A \subseteq X$ is *monotonic* if for every $s > s'$ and for every $t, (s', t) \in A$ implies $(s, t) \in A$ and $(t, s') \in A$ implies $(t, s) \in A$. In other words, a set is monotonic if, for every aspect, the higher its value, the better indication it is that the type is in A. The sets A in Examples 1 and 2 are monotonic whereas the sets A in Examples 4, 5, 6, and 7 are not.

The following proposition refers to the case in which the set of types is a continuum although it also gives some insight into the finite case:

Proposition 5.   *Let* $X = [0, 1] \times [0, 1]$, p *be uniform, and assume that* A *is monotonic and that* R *is closed, convex, and nonempty. Then there exists an optimal mechanism that is direct and deterministic with (sets of persuasive facts)* $V_k = [z_k, 1]$ *for some* $z_k > 0$ *for both* k.

Proof.   The mistake probability induced by the deterministic mechanisms with $V_k = [y_k, 1]$ is continuous in y_1 and y_2. Thus, there is an optimal mechanism within this class characterized by the sets of persuasive facts

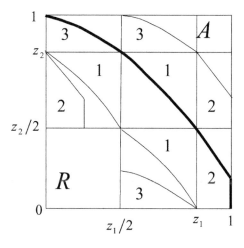

Figure 5.

$V_k = [z_k, 1]$. By our assumptions about R it must be that $z_k > 0$ for both k.

Assume first that $z_k < 1$ for both k. It follows from a modification of Proposition 4 that $z_2/2 = \max\{s|(z_1, s) \in R\}$ and $z_1/2 = \max\{s|(s, z_2) \in R\}$.

The rest of the proof extends the idea embedded in Example 1. In Figure 5 the set R is the area below the bold curve. The mistake probability induced by the mechanism above is the sum of the probabilities of the following three disjoint sets:

$$T_1 = \{(x_1, x_2) \in A | x_1 \leq z_1 \text{ and } x_2 \leq z_2\},$$
$$T_2 = \{(x_1, x_2) \in R | x_1 > z_1 \text{ and } x_2 \leq z_2/2\},$$
$$T_3 = \{(x_1, x_2) \in R | x_1 \leq z_1/2 \text{ and } x_2 > z_2\},$$

Note that by the convexity of R the sets

$$\{(x_1 - z_1/2, x_2)|(x_1, x_2) \in T_1\} \quad \text{and}$$
$$\{(x_1 - z_1, x_2 + z_2/2)|(x_1, x_2) \in T_2\}$$

have an empty intersection. Similarly,

$$\{(x_1, x_2 - z_2/2)|(x_1, x_2) \in T_1\} \quad \text{and}$$
$$\{(x_1 + z_1/2, x_2 - z_2)|(x_1, x_2) \in T_3\}$$

are disjoint. The collection of all sets

$$\{x, (x_1 - z_1/2, x_2), (x_1, x_2 - z_1/2)\} \quad \text{with } x \in T_1,$$
$$\{(x_1, x_2 + z_2/2), x, (x_1 - z_1, x_2 + z_2/2)\} \quad \text{with } x \in T_2, \quad \text{and}$$
$$\{(x_1 + z_1/2, x_2), x, (x_1 + z_1/2, x_2 - z_2)\} \quad \text{with } x \in T_3$$

is a collection of disjoint L's. Thus, the mistake probability induced by any mechanism must be at least the probability of $T_1 \cup T_2 \cup T_3$.

As to the case where $z_1 = z_2 = 1$ it must be that

$$\max\{s|(1, s) \in R\} \geq 1/2 \quad \text{and} \quad \max\{s|(s, 1) \in R\} \geq 1/2,$$

and thus the set A is a subset of $[1/2, 1] \times [1/2, 1]$. The mechanism "reject all" induces a mistake probability equal to the probability of the set A. Any mechanism induces a mistake probability at least as large as the probability of A since the collection of all sets $\{x, (x_1 - 1/2, x_2), (x_1, x_2 - 1/2)\}$ with $x \in A$, is a collection of disjoint L's.

Arguments similar to the above complete the proof for the case in which $z_k = 1$ for one k.   □

When the problem is monotonic but the set R is not convex, the optimal mechanism may not be deterministic. The following example is finite but could be extended to the case of a continuum.

Example 8. Let $X_1 = X_2 = \{1, 2, \ldots, 5\}$. The elements in R are indicated in Figure 6.

We will see that the optimal mechanism yields 4.5 mistakes and thus must be nondeterministic. Notice the six starred elements that produce three (nondisjoint) L's. Any mechanism that induces mistake probabilities

R*	*			*
R1			1	
R3	3			
R2	R*	2		*
R	R3	R2	R1	R*

Figure 6.

$(\mu_x)_{x \in X}$ must satisfy:

$$\mu_{5,5} + \mu_{1,5} + \mu_{5,1} \geq 1,$$
$$\mu_{2,5} + \mu_{2,2} + \mu_{1,5} \geq 1,$$
$$\mu_{5,2} + \mu_{2,2} + \mu_{5,1} \geq 1,$$

which implies that the sum of mistakes with respect to these six types must be at least 1.5. At least three additional mistakes must be induced with respect to the three disjoint L's indicated by the numbers 1, 2, and 3 in the figure. The fair random mechanism yields 4.5 mistakes (the 9 types in $R = \{(1,1)\}$ induce the action a with probability .5) and thus is optimal.

9. Related Literature

Our paper is related to the literature on strategic information transmission (see, for example, Crawford and Sobel (1982)). This literature studies a model in which a sender sends a costless message to a receiver. The listener cannot verify any of the information possessed by the sender. The interests of the sender and the receiver do not necessarily coincide. The situation is analyzed as a game and one of the questions asked is whether an informative sequential equilibrium exists. In contrast, the speaker in our model can choose to check some of the relevant information and the situation is analyzed as a mechanism design problem.

Some papers have studied principal agent problems in situations where the principal can obtain "hard evidence." In a very different context, Townsend (1979) studied the structure of efficient contracts in a model where the principal insures the agent against variability in the agent's wealth. The transfer of money from one party to the other may depend on the agent's wealth, which is initially known only to the agent. The principal can verify the agent's wealth if he incurs some cost. In this model the choice of the principal is whether or not to verify the state whereas in our model the focus is on the principal's choice of which aspect to check.

Some of the literature has studied the circumstances under which the revelation principle holds, whereas our main interest is in characterizing the optimal mechanisms.

Green and Laffont (1986) studies mechanisms in which the set of messages each type can send depends on the type and is a subset of the set of types. Their framework does not allow the listener to randomize. Furthermore, their model does not cover the case in which the speaker can show the value of the realization of one of the aspects. In particular, assuming in their framework that a type (i, j) can only send messages like (i, s) or (t, j) is not the same as assuming that he can present one of the aspects. The reason is that a message (m_1, m_2) would not reveal whether the agent actually showed that the realization of aspect 1 is m_1 or that he showed that the realization of aspect 2 is m_2.

In Bull and Watson (2002) an agent can also show some evidence. A key condition in their paper is what they call "normality": if type x can distinguish himself from type x' and from x'', then he can also distinguish himself from both, a condition that does not hold in our framework. Furthermore, they do not consider randomized mechanisms.

A related paper is Fishman and Hagerty (1990). One interpretation of what they do is the analysis of the optimal deterministic mechanisms for the problem $(\{0, 1\}^n, \{x \mid \sum_k x_k > b\})$ for some b.

Our own interest in this paper is rooted in Glazer and Rubinstein (2001) in which we study the design of optimal deterministic debate mechanisms in a specific example. (Other models of optimal design of debate rules with hard evidence are Shin (1994), Lipman and Seppi (1995), Deneckere and Severinov (2003), and Forges and Koessler (2003).) The two models are quite different but nevertheless have some common features. In both models there is a listener and speaker(s); the listener has to take an action after listening to arguments made by the speaker(s); an instance is characterized by the realization of several aspects and the speaker(s) knows the realization of the aspects while the listener does not; a constrained amount of "hard" evidence can be shown by the speaker(s) or checked by the listener; the listener must base his decision on only partial information. In both papers we look for a mechanism that minimizes the probability that the listener will take the wrong action.

References

Alon, N. (2003): "Problems and Results in Extremal Combinatorics — II," Mimeo.

Bull, J. and J. Watson (2002): "Hard Evidence and Mechanism Design," Working Paper.

Crawford, V. P. and J. Sobel (1982): "Strategic Information Transmission," *Econometrica*, 50, 1431–1451.

Deneckere, R. and S. Severinov (2003): "Mechanism Design and Communication Costs," Mimeo.

Fishman, M. J. and K. M. Hagerty (1990): "The Optimal Amount of Discretion to Allow in Disclosures," *Quarterly Journal of Economics*, 105, 427–444.

Forges, F. and F. Koessler (2003): "Communication Equilibria with Partially Verifiable Types," *Journal of Mathematical Economics*, forthcoming.

Glazer, J. and A. Rubinstein (2001): "Debates and Decisions, on a Rationale of Argumentation Rules," *Games and Economic Behavior,* 36, 158–173.

Green, J. and J. J. Laffont (1986): "Partially Verifiable Information and Mechanism Design," *Review of Economic Studies*, 53, 447–456.

Lipman, B. L. and D. J. Seppi (1995): "Robust Inference in Communication Games with Partial Provability," *Journal of Economic Theory*, 66, 370–405.

Shin, H. S. (1994): "The Burden of Proof in a Game of Persuasion," *Journal of Economic Theory*, 64, 253–264.

Townsend, R. (1979): "Optimal Contracts and Competitive Markets with Costly State Verification," *Journal of Economic Theory*, 21, 265–293.

Chapter 5

A Study in the Pragmatics of Persuasion: A Game Theoretical Approach

Jacob Glazer

Faculty of Management, Tel Aviv University
Department of Economics, Boston University
glazer@post.tau.ac.il

Ariel Rubinstein

School of Economics, Tel Aviv University
Department of Economics, New York University
rariel@post.tau.ac.il

A speaker wishes to persuade a listener to take a certain action. The conditions under which the request is justified, from the listener's point of view, depend on the state of the world, which is known only to the speaker. Each state is characterized by a set of statements from which the speaker chooses. A persuasion rule specifies which statements the listener finds persuasive. We study persuasion rules that maximize the probability that the listener accepts the request if and only if it is justified, given that the speaker maximizes the probability that his request is accepted. We prove that there always exists a persuasion rule involving no randomization and that all optimal persuasion rules are ex-post optimal. We relate our analysis to the field of pragmatics.

Keywords: Persuasion, mechanism design, hard evidence, pragmatics.

JEL Classification: C61, D82, D83.

1. Introduction

A persuasion situation involves an agent (*the speaker*) who attempts to persuade another agent (*the listener*) to take a certain action. Whether or not the listener should accept the speaker's suggestion depends on

---

We are grateful to an editor of this journal and anonymous referees for their thoughtful comments.

information possessed by the speaker. In such a situation, the speaker often presents hard evidence to support his position, but is restricted as to how many pieces of evidence he can present. This restriction may be due either to time constraints or to limitations on the listener's capability to process information. Our purpose in this paper is to shed light on the rules that determine which of the facts, presented by the speaker, the listener will find persuasive.

The topic of this paper is related to a field in linguistics called pragmatics, which explores the rules that determine how people interpret an utterance, made in the course of a conversation, beyond its literal content (see Grice 1989). Grice suggested that the leading principle in the interpretation of utterances is what he termed the "cooperative principle", according to which the interpretation of utterances in a regular conversation can be made on the assumption that the speaker and the listener have common interests. However, the cooperative principle does not appear to be relevant in a persuasion situation in which the agents may have conflicting interests.

The following example clarifies the distinction between the pragmatics of conversation and the pragmatics of persuasion: You are discussing the chances of each of two candidates in an upcoming election. The electorate consists of ten voters. Assume that the other person has access to the views of these ten voters. Imagine that he has just informed you that a, d, and g support candidate A. If it is a friendly conversation, then you are most likely to think that he has selected three people who represent the views of the majority of the voters. Thus, you are likely to be persuaded that A is likely to win the election. If, on the other hand, independently of the truth, the other person is trying to persuade you that A will win, you will find this very same statement to be a weak argument since you will suspect that he has intentionally selected three supporters of A.

What governs the pragmatic rules of persuasion? We propose an approach analogous to Grice's cooperative principle in which the pragmatic rules of persuasion are determined by a fictitious designer before the discourse begins. These rules govern the speaker's choice of facts to present in the knowledge that the listener will interpret his statements according to these rules. The rules are structured by the designer to maximize the probability that the listener will make the "right" decision (from his point of view and given the "true" situation) on the basis of the information provided to him by a self-interested speaker and subject to constraints on the amount of information that can be submitted to him by the speaker.

We conduct our investigation within the narrow boundaries of a particular model in which several assumptions admittedly play a critical role. Our analysis is faithful to economic tradition rather than to the methodology of Pragmatics. Nevertheless, we believe that the study conducted here demonstrates the potential of research to find a uniform principle that guides individuals in interpreting statements in persuasion situations.

This paper belongs to a research program in which we apply a game theoretical approach to issues in Pragmatics. In Glazer and Rubinstein (2001) we study an example of a debate situation involving two parties each of whom tries to persuade a third party to accept his position. Even closer to this paper is Glazer and Rubinstein (2004), which analyzes a persuasion situation in which after the speaker makes his case the listener can obtain partial information about the state of the world. After specifying our current model, we will compare it to the one in Glazer and Rubinstein (2004).

2. The Model

A speaker wishes to persuade a listener to take a certain action. The listener can either accept or reject the speaker's suggestion (there is no partial acceptance). Whether or not the listener should be persuaded depends on the *state*, which is an element in a set X. A set $A \subset X$ consists of all the states in which the listener would wish to be persuaded (i.e. to accept the speaker's suggestion) if he knew the state, and the set $R = X \backslash A$ consists of all the states in which the listener would wish to reject the speaker's request. The listener's initial beliefs about the state are given by a probability measure p over X. Denote by p_x the probability of state x.

We assume that for every state x, there is a set of statements $\sigma(x)$ that the speaker can make. Let $S = \cup_{x \in X} \sigma(x)$. The meaning of "making statement s" is to present proof that the event $\sigma^{-1}(s) = \{x | s \in \sigma(x)\}$ has occurred.

In state x the speaker can make one and only one of the statements in $\sigma(x)$. Thus, for example, if the speaker can choose between remaining silent, making the statement α, making the statement β, or making both statements, the set $\sigma(x)$ consists of the four elements *silence*, α, β, and $\alpha \wedge \beta$.

To summarize, we model a *persuasion problem* as a four-tuple $\langle X, A, p, \sigma \rangle$. We say that the persuasion problem is finite if X is finite. We refer to the pair $\langle X, \sigma \rangle$ as a *signal structure*.

Comment. We say that a signal structure $\langle Y, e \rangle$ is *vectoric* if Y is a product set, i.e. $Y = X_{k \in K} Y_k$ for some set K and some sets $Y_k, k \in K$, and the speaker in state x can make a statement concerning the value of one of the components of x, that is, $e(x) = \{(k, v) | k \in K \text{ and } v = x_k\}$.

One might think that we could make do by analyzing only vectoric signal structures. To see that this is not the case, let $\langle X, \sigma \rangle$ be a signal structure. Let $\langle Y, e \rangle$ be the vectoric signal structure with $Y = \{0, 1\}^S$. Every state $x \in X$ can be represented by the vector $\varphi(x) \in Y$, which indicates the statements available at x, that is, $\varphi(x)(s) = 1$ if $s \in \sigma(x)$ and 0 otherwise. However, the two structures are not equivalent. First, we allow for the possibility that two states have the same set of feasible statements. Second, and more importantly, in the corresponding vectoric structure the speaker in any state is able to show the value of the component that corresponds to any statement s. In other words, he is always able to prove whether s is available or not. In contrast, in our framework the fact that the speaker can make the statement s does not necessarily mean that he can make a statement that proves that s is not available.

We have in mind a situation in which the speaker makes a statement and the listener must then either take the action a, thus accepting the speaker's position, or the action r, thus rejecting it. A persuasion rule determines how the listener responds to each of the speaker's possible statements. We define a *persuasion rule* f as a function $f \colon S \to [0, 1]$. The function f specifies the speaker's beliefs about how the listener will interpret each of his possible statements. The meaning of $f(s) = q$ is that following a statement s, with probability q the listener is "persuaded" and chooses a, the speaker's favored action. We call a persuasion rule f *deterministic* if $f(s) \in \{0, 1\}$ for all $s \in S$.

We assume that the speaker wishes to maximize the probability that the listener is persuaded. Thus, given a state x, the speaker solves the problem $\max_{s \in \sigma(x)} f(s)$. The value of the solution, denoted by $\alpha(f, x)$, is the maximal probability of acceptance that the speaker can induce in state x. For the case in which $\sigma(x)$ is infinite, the solution can be approached but is not attainable and therefore we define $\alpha(f, x) = \sup_{s \in \sigma(x)} f(s)$.

Given the assumption that the speaker maximizes the probability of acceptance, we define the (listener's) error probability $\mu_x(f)$ in state x as follows: If $x \in A$, then $\mu_x(f) = 1 - \alpha(f, x)$, and if $x \in R$, then $\mu_x(f) = \alpha(f, x)$. The *error probability* induced by the persuasion rule f is $m(f) = \sum_{x \in X} p_x \mu_x(f)$. Given a problem $\langle X, A, p, \sigma \rangle$, an *optimal* persuasion rule is one that minimizes $m(f)$.

Note that persuasion rules are evaluated according to the listener's interests while those of the speaker are ignored. In addition, we assume that all errors are treated symmetrically. Our analysis remains the same if we add a variable c_x for the (listener's) "costs" of an error in state x and define the objective function to minimize $\sum_{x \in X} p_x c_x \mu_x(f)$.

Example 1 ("The majority of the facts supports my position").
There are five independent random variables, each of which takes the values 1 and 0 each with probability 0.5. A realization of 1 means that the random variable supports the speaker's position. The listener would like to accept the speaker's position if and only if at least three random variables take the value 1. In the process of persuasion, the speaker can present the realization of at most m random variables that support his position.

Formally, $X = \{(x_1, \ldots, x_5)|x_k \in \{0,1\} \text{ for all } k\}, A = \{x|n(x) \geq 3\}$ where $n(x) = \sum_k x_k, p_x = \frac{1}{32}$ for all $x \in X$, and $\sigma(x) = \{\kappa|\kappa \subseteq \{k|x_k = 1\}$ and $|\kappa| \leq m\}$.

If $m = 3$, the optimal persuasion rule states that the listener is persuaded if the speaker presents any three random variables that take the value 1. The more interesting case is $m = 2$. If the listener is persuaded by the presentation of any two random variables that support the speaker's position, then the error probability is $\frac{10}{32}$. The persuasion rule according to which the listener is persuaded only by the speaker presenting a set of two "neighboring" random variables ($\{1,2\}, \{2,3\}, \{3,4\}$, or $\{4,5\}$) with the value 1 reduces the error probability to $\frac{5}{32}$ (an error in favor of the speaker occurs in the four states in which exactly two neighboring random variables support the speaker's position and in the state $(1,0,1,0,1)$ in which the speaker is not able to persuade the listener to support him even though he should).

The two mechanisms above do not use lotteries. Can the listener do better by applying a random mechanism? What is the optimal mechanism in that case? We return to this example after presenting some additional results.

Comment. At this point, we wish to compare the current model with the one studied in Glazer and Rubinstein (2004). Both models deal with a persuasion situation in which (a) the speaker attempts to persuade the listener to take a particular action and (b) only the speaker knows the state of the world and therefore whether or not the listener should accept the speaker's request.

Unlike the current model, the speaker in the previous model could first send an arbitrary message (cheap talk) to the listener. After receiving the message, the listener could ask the speaker to present some hard evidence to support his request. The state of the world in that model is a realization of two random variables and the listener is able to ask the speaker to reveal at most one of them. Thus, unlike the current model, in which the speaker simply decides which hard evidence to present, in the previous model the speaker has to "follow the listener's instructions" and the listener can apply a random device to determine which hard evidence he asks the speaker to present. That randomization was shown to often be a critical element in the listener's optimal persuasion rule (a point further discussed below). On the other hand, in the previous model we do not allow randomization during the stage in which the listener finally decides whether or not to accept the speaker's request, which we do allow in the current model. Allowing for such randomization in the previous model, however, is not beneficial to the listener, as we show to be the case in the current paper as well.

The randomization in the previous paper is employed during the stage in which the listener has to decide which hard evidence to request from the speaker. Note that if in that model we restrict attention to deterministic persuasion rules, then it is a special case of the current model. Eliminating randomization on the part of the listener in order to verify the information presented by the speaker, allows us to think about the persuasion situation in the previous model as one in which the speaker chooses which hard evidence to present rather than one in which the listener chooses which hard evidence to request.

Randomization plays such an important role in the previous model because it is, in fact, employed as a verification device. Without randomization, there is no value to the speaker's message since he could be lying. The listener uses randomization to induce the speaker to transfer more information than the information that is eventually verified.

Although the current model draws some inspiration from the previous one, the two papers relate to different persuasion situations and the results of the current paper cannot be derived from those of the previous one.

3. Two Lemmas

We now present two lemmas that are useful in deriving an optimal persuasion rule.

3.1. *A finite number of persuasive statements is sufficient*

Our first observation is rather technical though simple. We show that if the set of states X is finite then even if the set of statements S is infinite there is an optimal persuasion rule in which at most $|X|$ statements are persuasive with positive probability.

Lemma 1.   *Let $\langle X, A, p, \sigma \rangle$ be a finite persuasion problem.*

(*i*) *An optimal persuasion rule exists.*
(*ii*) *There is an optimal persuasion rule in which $\{s | f(s) > 0\}$ does not contain more than $|X|$ elements.*

Proof.   Consider a partition of S such that s and s' are in the same cell of the partition if $\sigma^{-1}(s) = \sigma^{-1}(s')$. This partition is finite. Let T be a set of statements consisting of one statement from each cell of the partition. We now show that for every persuasion rule f, there is a persuasion rule g that takes a positive value only on T, such that $\alpha(g, x) = \alpha(f, x)$ for all x and thus $m(g) = m(f)$.

For every $s \in T$ let S_s be the cell in the partition of S that contains s. Define $g(s) = \sup_{s' \in S_s} f(s')$. For every $s \notin T$ define $g(s) = 0$.

For every state x,

$$\alpha(g, x) = \max_{s \in T \cap \sigma(x)} g(s) = \max_{s \in T \cap \sigma(x)} \sup_{s' \in S_s} f(s') = \sup_{s' \in \sigma(x)} f(s') = \alpha(f, x).$$

Thus, we can confine ourselves to persuasion rules that take the value 0 for any statement besides those in the finite set T. Any such persuasion rule is characterized by a vector in the compact set $[0, 1]^T$. The error probability is a continuous function on this space and thus there is an optimal persuasion rule f^* with $f^*(s) = 0$ for all $s \notin T$.

For every $x \in S$ let $s(x) \in \sigma(x)$ be a solution of $\max_{s \in \sigma(x)} f^*(s)$. Let g^* be a persuasion rule such that

$$g^*(s) = \begin{cases} f^*(s) & \text{if } s = s(x) \text{ for some } x \\ 0 & \text{otherwise.} \end{cases}$$

The persuasion rule g^* is optimal as well since $\alpha(g^*, x) = \alpha(f^*, x)$ for all x and thus $m(g^*) = m(f^*)$. Thus, we can confine ourselves to persuasion rules for which the number of statements that persuade the listener with positive probability is no larger than the size of the state space.   □

3.2. The "L-principle"

The following result is based on an idea discussed in Glazer and Rubinstein (2004).

Let $\langle X, A, p, \sigma \rangle$ be a persuasion problem such that for all $x \in X, \sigma(x)$ is finite. We say that a pair (x, T), where $x \in A$ and $T \subseteq R$, is an L if for any $s \in \sigma(x)$ there is $t \in T$ such that $s \in \sigma(t)$. That is, an L consists of an element x in A and a set T of elements in R such that every statement that can be made by x can also be made by some member of T. An $L, (x, T)$ is minimal if there is no $T' \subset T$ such that (x, T') is an L.

Lemma 2 (The L-Principle). *Let (x, T) be an L in the persuasion problem $\langle X, A, p, \sigma \rangle$ and let f be a persuasion rule. Then $\sum_{t \in \{x\} \cup T} \mu_t(f) \geq 1$.*

Proof.   Recall that $\mu_x(f) = 1 - \alpha(f, x)$ and for every $t \in T, \mu_t(f) = \alpha(f, t)$. Therefore,

$$\sum_{t \in \{x\} \cup T} \mu_t(f) \geq \mu_x(f) + \max_{t \in T} \mu_t(f) \geq \mu_x(f) + \max_{s \in \sigma(x)} f(s)$$

$$= \mu_x(f) + \alpha(f, x) = 1.$$

$\square$

The following example demonstrates how the L-principle can be used to verify that a certain persuasion rule is optimal. For any persuasion problem, the L-principle provides a lower bound on the probability of error that can be induced by a persuasion rule. Thus, if a particular persuasion rule induces a probability of error equal to a lower bound derived from the L-principle, then one can conclude that this persuasion rule is optimal.

Example 2 ("I have outperformed the population average"). Consider a situation in which a speaker wishes to persuade a listener that his average performance in two previous tasks was above the average performance of the population. Denote by x_1 the proportion of the population that performed worse than the speaker in the first task and by x_2 the proportion of the population that performed worse than the speaker in the second task. The speaker wishes to persuade the listener that $x_1 + x_2 \geq 1$. The speaker knows his relative performance in the two tasks (that is, he knows x_1 and x_2) but can present details of his performance in only one of the tasks. We assume that the speaker's performances in the two tasks are uncorrelated. Formally, the signal structure is vectoric with $X = [0,1] \times [0,1]$; the probability measure p is uniform on X; and $A = \{(x_1, x_2)|x_1 + x_2 \geq 1\}$.

Note that if a statement is interpreted by the listener based only on its content, i.e. by stating that his performance was above $\frac{1}{2}$ in one of the tasks, the speaker persuades the listener and the probability of error is $\frac{1}{4}$.

The following argument (borrowed from Glazer and Rubinstein 2004) shows that there exists an optimal persuasion rule according to which the listener is persuaded by the speaker if and only if the speaker can show that his performance in one of the two tasks was above $\frac{2}{3}$. Furthermore, the minimal probability of error is $\frac{1}{6}$.

A minimal L in this case is any pair $(x, \{y, z\})$ where $x \in A, y, z \in R$, $x_1 = y_1$, and $x_2 = z_2$.

The set $T_1 = \{(x_1, x_2) \in A | x_1 \leq \frac{2}{3} \text{ and } x_2 \leq \frac{2}{3}\}$ is one of the three triangles denoted in Figure 1 by the number 1. Any three points $x = (x_1, x_2) \in T_1, y = (x_1 - \frac{1}{3}, x_2) \in R$ and $z = (x_1, x_2 - \frac{1}{3}) \in R$ establish an L. By the L-principle, for any persuasion rule f we have $\mu_x(f) + \mu_y(f) + \mu_z(f) \geq 1$. The collection of all these L's is a set of disjoint sets whose union is the three triangles denoted in the figure by the number 1. Therefore, the integral of $\mu_x(f)$ over these three triangles must be at least the size of T_1, namely $\frac{1}{18}$. Similar considerations regarding the three triangles denoted by the number 2 and the three triangles denoted by the number 3 imply that the minimal error probability is at least $\frac{1}{6}$. This error probability is attained by the persuasion rule according to which the

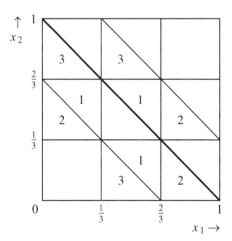

Figure 1.   An optimal persuasion rule for Example 2.

listener is persuaded if and only if the speaker shows that either x_1 or x_2 take a value of at least $\frac{2}{3}$.

4. Randomization is Not Needed

The next question to be addressed is whether randomization has any role in the design of the optimal persuasion rule. In other words, can the listener ever do better by making the speaker uncertain about the consequences of his statement? Glazer and Rubinstein (2004) show that in persuasion situations in which the listener can acquire partial information about the state of the world, uncertainty regarding what information he will acquire can be a useful device to the listener. However, as stated in Proposition 1 below, uncertainty is not useful to the listener in the present context.

Proposition 1. (*i*) *For every finite persuasion problem* $\langle X, A, p, \sigma \rangle$, *there exists an optimal persuasion rule f that is deterministic.*

(*ii*) *For every persuasion problem* $\langle X, A, p, \sigma \rangle$ *and every* $\epsilon > 0$, *there exists a deterministic persuasion rule f^* such that* $m(f^*) < \inf_f m(f) + \epsilon$.

Proof. (i) By Lemma 1, there exists an optimal persuasion rule with a finite number of statements that induces acceptance with positive probability. Consider an optimal persuasion rule f with the fewest non-integer values. Let $0 < \alpha_1 < \cdots \alpha_K < 1$ be the values of f that are not 0 or 1. We show that $K = 0$. If not, consider the set $T = \{s | f(s) = \alpha_1\}$. Let Y be the set of all states in which it is optimal for the speaker to make a statement from T, that is, $Y = \{x | \alpha(f, x) = \alpha_1\}$.

If the probability of $Y \cap A$ is at least that of $Y \cap R$, then consider f^+ which is a revision of f:

$$f^+(s) = \alpha_2 \text{ for all } s \in T \quad \text{and} \quad f^+(s) = f(s) \text{ for } s \notin T.$$

Thus, $\alpha(f^+, x) = \alpha_2$ for $x \in Y$ and $\alpha(f^+, x) = \alpha(f, x)$ for $x \notin Y$. It follows that $m(f^+) \leq m(f)$.

If the probability of $Y \cap A$ is at most that of $Y \cap R$, then consider f^- which is a revision of f:

$$f^-(s) = 0 \text{ for all } s \in T \quad \text{and} \quad f^-(s) = f(s) \text{ for } s \notin T.$$

Thus, $\alpha(f^-, x) = 0$ for $x \in Y$ and $\alpha(f^-, x) = \alpha(f, x)$ for $x \notin Y$. It follows that $m(f^-) \leq m(f)$.

The number of non-integer values used by either f^+ or f^- is reduced by 1, which contradicts the assumption that f uses the the minimal number of non-integer values.

(ii) Let f' be a persuasion rule such that $m(f') < \inf_f m(f) + \epsilon/2$. Let n be an integer such that $1/n < \epsilon/2$. Let f'' be the persuasion rule defined by $f''(s) = \max\{m/n | m/n \leq f'(s)\}$. Obviously $m(f'') < m(f') + 1/n$. The persuasion rule f'' involves a finite number of values. By the proof of Proposition 1 there is a deterministic persuasion rule f^* with $m(f^*) \leq m(f'')$. Thus, $m(f^*) < m(f') + \epsilon/2 < \inf_f m(f) + \epsilon$. ☐

Example 1 Revisited: A solution. We return now to Example 1 and show that no persuasion rule induces a probability of error less than $\frac{4}{32}$. Consider an optimal persuasion rule that is deterministic. Thus, μ_x is either 0 or 1 for any state x. By the L-principle, $\mu(1,1,1,0,0) + \mu(1,1,0,0,0) + \mu(1,0,1,0,0) + \mu(0,1,1,0,0) \geq 1$ and similar inequalities hold for any of the other 9 states in which exactly three aspects support the speaker. Summing up over these 10 inequalities yields

$$\sum_{n(x)=3} \mu_x + 3 \sum_{n(x)=2} \mu_x \geq 10$$

Using the fact that μ_x is either 0 or 1 implies that $\sum_{n(x)=3} \mu_x + \sum_{n(x)=2} \mu_x \geq 4$ and thus $\sum_x p_x \mu_x \geq \frac{4}{32}$.

Let us now describe an optimal persuasion rule for this case. Partition the set of random variables into the two sets $\{1,2,3\}$ and $\{4,5\}$. The listener is persuaded only if the speaker can show that two random variables from the same cell of the partition support him. In states in which there are at least three random variables in favor of the speaker, at least two of them must belong to the same cell and, thus, the speaker is justifiably able to persuade the listener. However, in the four states in which exactly two random variables belonging to the same cell support the speaker's position, the speaker is able to persuade the listener even though he should not be able to. Thus, the probability of error under this persuasion rule is $\frac{4}{32}$.

This persuasion rule seems to be attractive when the partition of the random variables is prominent. For example, if the random variables are associated with Alice, Beth, Christina, Dan, and Edward, they can naturally be divided into two groups by gender. Given the constraint that the speaker cannot refer to more than two individuals, we have found an optimal persuasion rule whereby referring to two individuals of the same gender is more persuasive than referring to two individuals of different gender.

Example 3 (Persuading someone that the median is above the expected value). A speaker wishes to persuade the listener that the median of the values of three independent random variables uniformly distributed over the interval $[0,1]$ is above 0.5. The speaker can reveal the value of only one of the three random variables. Is it more persuasive to present a random variable with a realization of 0.9 or one with a realization of 0.6?

Formally, let $X = [0,1] \times [0,1] \times [0,1]$ with a uniform distribution and $A = \{(x_1, x_2, x_3)| \text{ two of the values are above } 0.5\}$. Let $x_i = t_i$ denote the statement "the realization of the variable x_i is t_i" and $S(t_1, t_2, t_3) = \{x_1 = t_1, x_2 = t_2, x_3 = t_3\}$. In other words $\langle X, S \rangle$ is vectoric.

The persuasion rule according to which the listener is persuaded only by the statement $x_1 = t_1$ where $t_1 > \frac{1}{2}$ yields a probability of error of $\frac{1}{4}$. We will employ the L-principle to show that this persuasion rule is optimal.

Note that the space X is isomorphic to the probabilistic space $Y \times Z$ with a uniform distribution, where $Y = [0, \frac{1}{2}] \times [0, \frac{1}{2}] \times [0, \frac{1}{2}]$ and $Z = \{-1, 1\} \times \{-1, 1\} \times \{-1, 1\}$, by identifying a pair (y, z) with $x = (\frac{1}{2} + y_i z_i)_{i=1,2,3}$.

As a result, every $(y, (1, 1, -1)) \in A$ is a part of an L with $(y, (-1, 1, -1)) \in R$ and $(y, (1, -1, -1)) \in R$.

Thus we obtain the following inequalities:

$$\mu_{(y,(1,1,-1))} + \mu_{(y,(-1,1,-1))} + \mu_{(y,(1,-1,-1))} \geq 1$$

$$\mu_{(y,(1,-1,1))} + \mu_{(y,(-1,-1,1))} + \mu_{(y,(1,-1,-1))} \geq 1$$

$$\mu_{(y,(-1,1,1))} + \mu_{(y,(-1,1,-1))} + \mu_{(y,(-1,-1,1))} \geq 1.$$

Hence

$$\mu_{(y,(1,1,-1))} + \mu_{(y,(1,-1,1))} + \mu_{(y,(-1,1,1))}$$
$$+ 2\mu_{(y,(-1,1,-1))} + 2\mu_{(y,(1,-1,-1))} + 2\mu_{(y,(-1,-1,1))} \geq 3.$$

For deterministic persuasion rules it must be that at least two of the variables $\mu_{(y,z)}$ take the value 1 and, thus, for all y, we have $\sum_z p_{(y,z)} \mu_{(y,z)} \geq \frac{2}{8} = \frac{1}{4}$. If there exists a persuasion rule that yields an error probability strictly less than $\frac{1}{4}$, then by Proposition 1(ii) there is also a deterministic persuasion rule that yields an error probability less than $\frac{1}{4}$. Thus, the persuasion rule described above (which yields an error probability of exactly $\frac{1}{4}$) is optimal.

5. A Procedure for Finding an Optimal Persuasion Rule

We are now able to prove a proposition that reduces the task of finding an optimal persuasion rule to a simple optimization problem.

Proposition 2. *Let $\langle X, A, p, \alpha \rangle$ be a finite persuasion problem. Let $(\mu_x^*)_{x \in X}$ be a solution to the optimization problem*

$$\min_{\{\mu_x\}_{x \in X}} \sum_{x \in X} p_x \mu_x \ s.t. \ \mu_x \in \{0,1\} \ for \ all \ x \in X \quad and$$

$$\sum_{t \in \{x\} \cup T} \mu_t \geq 1 \ for \ any \ minimal \ L, (x, T).$$

Then there is an optimal persuasion rule that induces the probabilities of error $(\mu_x^*)_{x \in X}$.

Proof. By Proposition 1 we can restrict ourselves to deterministic mechanisms. By Lemma 2 any persuasion rule satisfies the constraints (regarding the L's), so it is sufficient to construct a persuasion rule f that induces the optimal error probabilities vector $(\mu_x^*)_{x \in X}$.

Define $f(s) = 1$ for any signal s such that there exist $x \in A$ with $s \in \sigma(x)$ so that $\mu_x^* = 0$ and $\mu_y^* = 1$ for all $y \in R$ with $s \in \sigma(y)$. Define $f(s) = 0$ for any other signal s.

It is sufficient to show that for all x, the induced probability $\mu_x(f) \leq \mu_x^*$.

Let $x \in A$ and $\mu_x^* = 0$. There is a statement $s_x \in \sigma(x)$ so that $\mu_y^* = 1$ for all $y \in R$ such that $s_x \in \sigma(y)$. Otherwise, there is an $L, (x, T)$ such that $\sum_{t \in \{x\} \cup T} \mu_t^* = 0$. Thus $f(s_x) = 1$ and $\mu_x(f) = 0$.

Let $x \in R$ and $\mu_x^* = 0$. Then there is no $s \in \sigma(x)$ such that $f(s) = 1$ and thus $\alpha(f, x) = 0$ and $\mu_x(f) = \mu_x^*$. $\square$

6. Ex-post Optimality

So far we have assumed that the listener is committed to a persuasion rule. In what follows, we address the question of whether the listener's optimal persuasion rule is one that he would indeed follow were he able to reconsider his commitment after the speaker has made his statement.

To motivate this analysis consider the following example.

Example 4. The listener wishes to choose a guest for a TV news program. He is looking for a person with strong views about the issues of the day. There is a potential candidate who the listener knows is one of four types: "hawk" (H), "dove" (D), a "pretender" (M) who can pretend to be either a hawk or a dove, or "ignorant" (I). The listener is not interested in the candidate's political views, but only in whether he has clear views one way or the other, i.e., if he is type H or D. The probabilities of the types are $p(H) = p(D) = 0.2$ and $p(M) = p(I) = 0.3$.

The listener can interview the candidate, after which he must decide whether or not to invite him onto the show. During the interview the listener plans to ask the speaker to make a statement regarding his views on current issues. Assume that apart from remaining silent (action 0), type H can make only the statement h; D can make only the statement d; and M can make either statement h or d. Type I can only remain silent. Thus, $\sigma(H) = \{h, 0\}, \sigma(D) = \{d, 0\}, \sigma(M) = \{h, d, 0\}$, and $\sigma(I) = \{0\}$.

A "naive" approach to this problem is the following: Given the statement s, the listener excludes the types that cannot make the statement s and makes the optimal decision given the probabilities. For example, the message d excludes types I and H and therefore implies that the conditional probability that the speaker is of type D is 0.4. The listener thus rejects the speaker. This approach yields a probability of error of 0.4.

Suppose that the listener can commit to how he will respond to the speaker's statement. It is easy to see that, in this example, the listener can reduce the probability of error to 0.3. The best persuasion rule is to invite the speaker to the show if and only if he makes the statement d or h. (This avoids the possibility that I is invited to the show but leaves the possibility that, in addition to H and D, M might be invited.).

Assume now that the listener is released from his commitment once a statement has been made. If he believes that M's strategy is to utter d, then the listener, upon hearing the statement d, should attribute a higher probability to the possibility that he is facing M than to the possibility that he is facing D. Therefore, in this case he should not follow the optimal persuasion rule and should reject the speaker if he makes the statement d. If, however, the listener believes that M randomizes with equal probability between uttering d and h, then the listener, upon hearing the message $d(h)$, should attribute the probability $\frac{4}{7}$ to the possibility that he is facing type $D(H)$ and, thus, should not deviate from the optimal persuasion rule.

Note that the ex-post optimality of the optimal persuasion rule in this example hinges on the knife-edge condition that the speaker of type M randomizes with equal probability between h and d. This observation hints at the possibility that a persuasion problem might exist in which the listener's optimal persuasion rule is not ex-post optimal. However, as the analysis below demonstrates, this is never the case for finite persuasion problems.

For a given persuasion problem $\langle X, A, p, \sigma \rangle$, consider the corresponding extensive persuasion game $\Gamma(X, A, p, \sigma)$. First, nature chooses the state according to p; the speaker is then informed of the state x and makes a statement from the set $\sigma(x)$; and finally, after hearing the speaker's statement, the listener chooses between a and r. The payoff for the speaker is 1 if the listener takes the action a and 0 otherwise. The payoff for the listener is 1 if $x \in A$ and the action a is taken or if $x \in R$ and the action r is taken, and 0 otherwise. We say that a persuasion rule f is *credible* if there exists a sequential equilibrium of $\Gamma(X, A, p, \sigma)$ such that the listener's strategy is f.

Example 2 Revisited. The optimal persuasion rule described above is credible. The speaker's strategy of arguing in state (t_1, t_2) that $x_1 = t_1$ if $t_1 \geq t_2$ and that $x_2 = t_2$ if $t_2 > t_1$ is optimal. The set of types that use the argument $x_1 = t_1$ is $\{(t_1, x_2) | x_2 \leq t_1\}$. Conditional on this set, the probability that (t_1, x_2) is in A is greater than $\frac{1}{2}$ if and only if $t_1 > \frac{2}{3}$ and is less than $\frac{1}{2}$ if and only if $t_1 < \frac{2}{3}$.

Proposition 3. *If the persuasion problem is finite, then any optimal persuasion rule is credible.*

This proposition follows from solving the auxiliary problem presented in the next section.

Comment. The problem studied here can be viewed as a special case of a leader-follower problem in which the leader can commit to his future moves. As is well known, it is generally not true that the solution to such an optimization problem is credible. We are not aware, however, of any general theorem or principle that addresses this issue and that can explain why it is the case that in our model the listener's optimal strategy is credible. This question remains for future research.

We should emphasize, however, that Proposition 3 does not hold in the case that the listener has three actions, the speaker holds a fixed ordering over the actions, and the listener's preferences depend on the state. Consider, for example, the case in which the set of states is $X = \{1, 2\}$, the probability measure over X is $p_1 = 0.4$ and $p_2 = 0.6$, the signal function is $\sigma(1) = \{1\}, \sigma(2) = \{1, 2\}$, and the listener's set of actions is $\{1, 2, 3\}$. The speaker always prefers 1 over 2 and 2 over 3 and the listener's utility from the state x and action a is $u(1,1) = u(2,2) = 1, u(1,2) = u(2,1) = -1$, and $u(1,3) = u(2,3) = 0$. The optimal persuasion rule for the listener is to respond to signal 2 with action 2 and to signal 1 with action 3. However, once he observes signal 1 it is better for the listener to take action 1.

7. The Bridges Problem

A group of individuals is partitioned into a finite number of types, which are members of a set X. The mass of type x is p_x. Let S be a set of bridges spanning a river. The individuals are located on one side of the river and would like to cross to the other side.

Individuals of type $x \in X$ can use only the bridges in the set $\sigma(x) \neq \emptyset$. The set X is partitioned into two subsets, A whose members are welcome on the other side and R whose members are not. A decision maker has to decide, for each bridge, the probability that that bridge will be open. The decision maker cannot discriminate between the individuals in A and R. Each individual of type x chooses a bridge in $\sigma(x)$ with the highest probability of being open from among the ones he can use. The decision maker's objective is to maximize the "net flow", i.e., the difference in size between the group of type A's and the group of type R's crossing the river.

A bridge policy determines the probability with which each bridge is open. A bridge policy is credible if there exists an assignment of types to bridges whereby: (i) each type is assigned only to a bridge he can use, (ii) within the set of bridges he can use, each type is assigned only to bridges with the highest probability of being open, and (iii) the mass of types in A who are assigned to a bridge that is open (closed) with strictly positive probability is at least as high (low) as the mass of types in R who are assigned to that bridge. We show that any optimal bridge policy is credible.

Formally, a *bridge policy* is a function $O: S \rightarrow [0,1]$ with the interpretation that $O(s)$ is the probability that bridge s is open. Let $\alpha(O,x) = \max\{O(s) \mid s \in \sigma(x)\}$, that is the maximal probability of crossing the bridges that type x can achieve given the bridge policy O. Let $N(O) = \sum_{x \in A} p_x \alpha(O,x) - \sum_{x \in R} p_x \alpha(O,x)$ be called the net flow. A bridge policy is *optimal* if it maximizes $N(O)$. Given a bridge policy O, a *rational feasible bridge assignment* β is a function that assigns to each type x a probability measure on $\sigma(x)$, such that $\beta(x)(s) > 0$ only for values of s that maximize $O(s)$ in $\sigma(x)$. Given an assignment β, the *net assignment* to bridge s is $n(s,\beta) = \sum_{x \in A} p_x \beta(x)(s) - \sum_{x \in R} p_x \beta(x)(s)$. A bridge policy O is *credible* if there is a rational feasible assignment β such that for every $s, O(s) > 0$ implies $n(s, \beta) \geq 0$ and $O(s) < 1$ implies $n(s, \beta) \leq 0$.

Claim 1. *All optimal bridge policies are credible.*

Proof. Let O^* be an optimal bridge policy. For any assignment β, let

$$\delta(\beta) = \sum_{s \in \{s | n(s,\beta) < 0\}} |n(s, \beta)| O^*(s) + \sum_{s \in \{s | n(s,\beta) > 0\}} n(s, \beta)(1 - O^*(s)).$$

Let β^* be a minimizer of $\delta(\beta)$ over all rational feasible assignments. We show that $\delta(\beta^*) = 0$ and thus for all s such that $O^*(s) > 0$ we have $n(s, \beta) \geq 0$ and for all s that $O^*(s) < 1$ we have $n(s, \beta) \leq 0$.

Assume, for the purpose of contradiction, that $\delta(\beta^*) > 0$. Assume that there is a bridge s for which $O^*(s) > 0$ and $n(s, \beta^*) < 0$ (an analogous argument applies to the case in which there is a bridge s for which $O^*(s) < 1$ and $n(s, \beta^*) > 0$).

Let α be the minimum of $O^*(s)$ over $\{s | O^*(s) > 0$ and $n(s, \beta^*) < 0\}$. Let $S(\alpha) = \{s | O^*(s) = \alpha\}$. Let $X(\alpha) = \{x | \beta^*(x)(s) > 0$ for a bridge s such that $s \in S(\alpha)\}$, that is, $X(\alpha)$ is the set of types who are assigned by β^* to the bridges whose probability of being open is α. Note that types in $X(\alpha)$ cannot do better than trying to cross a bridge in $S(\alpha)$ and are indifferent between all bridges in $S(\alpha)$. Let $S_0 = \{s \in S(\alpha) | n(s, \beta^*) < 0\}$. The set S_0 is not empty and contains all bridges that are open with probability α and for which the net assignment is negative.

Let $y_1, \ldots, y_T$ be the longest sequence of distinct bridges in $S(\alpha) - S_0$ such that for every y_t,

(i) $n(y_t, \beta^*) = 0$
(ii) there exist $x \in R$ and $y_0 \in S_0 \cup \{y_1, \ldots, y_{t-1}\}$ such that $\beta^*(x)(y_0) > 0$ and $y_t \in \sigma(x)$.

In other words, under β^* each y_t is a bridge with a zero net transfer such that there is a positive mass of types in R that can cross y_t and is assigned by β^* either to cross a bridge that precedes y_t in the sequence or to cross a bridge in S_0.

Denote $Z = S_0 \cup \{y_1, \ldots, y_T\}$. There are two possibilities:

(i) There is no $s \in S(\alpha) - Z$, $x \in R$, and $z \in Z$ such that $s \in \sigma(x)$ and $\beta^*(x)(z) > 0$. That is, there is no bridge s outside Z that is open with probability α and that can be crossed by a type in R who can cross the river with probability α. The net transfer in Z is negative. Reducing the probability of transfer to all bridges in Z will increase the total net flow, thus violating the optimally of O^*.

(ii) There is $s \in S(\alpha) - Z, x \in R$, and $z \in Z$ such that $s \in \sigma(x)$ and $\beta^*(x)(z) > 0$. By the definition of $(y_1, \ldots, y_T)$ it must be that $n(s, \beta^*) > 0$. It follows that there are sequences of distinct bridges $s_0, s_1, \ldots, s_K = s$ and types $i_0, \ldots, i_{K-1} \in R$ such that $s_0 \in S_0$, $\beta^*(i_k)(s_k) > 0$, and $s_{k+1} \in \sigma(i_k)$ (for $k = 0, \ldots, K - 1$). This allows us to construct a new rational assignment β by shifting a positive mass of types in R from s_0 to s_1, from s_1 to s_2, and so on, such that $\delta(\beta) < \delta(\beta^*)$. Formally, let ε be a positive number such that for $k = 0, \ldots, K - 1$ we have $\varepsilon < \beta^*(i_k)(s_k), \varepsilon < n(s_K, \beta^*)$, and $\varepsilon < |n(s_0, \beta^*)|$. Define β to be an assignment that is obtained from β^* by successively shifting to s_{k+1} a mass ε of individuals of type i_k assigned by β^* to cross s_k. For all bridges with the exception of s_0 and s_K we have $n(s, \beta) = n(s, \beta^*)$. Furthermore, $n(s_K, \beta) = n(s_K, \beta^*) - \varepsilon > 0$ and $n(s_0, \beta) = n(s_0, \beta^*) + \varepsilon < 0$. Thus, $\delta(\beta) = \delta(\beta^*) - \alpha\varepsilon - (1 - \alpha)\varepsilon$, contradicting the choice of β^*.

Thus, it follows that there exists a rational feasible assignment with nonnegative net flow on all open bridges and nonpositive net flow on all closed bridges.   □

8. Concluding Remarks

This paper has attempted to make a modest contribution to the growing literature linking economic theory to linguistics. Our purpose is not to suggest a general theory for the pragmatics of persuasion but rather to demonstrate a rationale for inferences in persuasion situations.

One of our main findings is that any optimal persuasion rule is also ex-post optimal. It is quite rare that in a principal-agent problem the optimal incentive scheme is one that the principal would wish to obey even after the agent has made his move. The bridge problem described in Section 7 provides an example of a principal-agent problem that in fact does have this property. The problem discussed in Glazer and Rubinstein (2004) is shown there to have this property as well. The generalizability of this result is still an open question.

Our work is related to several areas of research in linguistics and economics. In the linguistics literature, our paper belongs to the emerging field that tries to explain pragmatic rules by employing game theoretical methods. In our approach, pragmatic rules determine a game between the participants in the discourse. Whatever the process that created these rules, it is of interest to compare them with the rules that would have been chosen by a rational designer seeking to maximize the functionality of the discourse. Such an approach is suggested in Glazer and Rubinstein (2001, 2004) and discussed in Rubinstein (2000). A recent collection of articles in Benz et al. (2006) presents various ideas that explain pragmatics phenomena using game theoretical tools.

Within the economic literature our paper is related to two areas of research.

The first investigates sender-receiver games (see Crawford and Sobel 1982) in which one agent (the sender) sends a costless message to the other (the receiver). The receiver cannot verify any of the information sent by the sender and the interests of the sender and the receiver do not necessarily coincide. The typical question in this literature is whether an informative sequential equilibrium exists.

The second (and closer) area of research studies models where a principal tries to elicit verifiable information from the agent(s). The agent however can choose which pieces of information to convey. Among the early papers on this topic are Townsend (1979), Green and Laffont (1986), and Milgrom and Roberts (1986), and among the more recent are Bull and Watson (2004), Deneckere and Severinov (2003), Fishman and Hagerty (1990), Forges and Koessler (2005), Lipman and Seppi (1995), and Shin (1994).

References

Benz, Anton, Gerhard Jäger, and Robert van Rooij (eds.) (2006), *Game Theory and Pragmatics*. Palgrave Macmillan, Basingstoke. [409]

Bull, Jesse and Joel Watson (2004), "Evidence disclosure and verifiability." *Journal of Economic Theory*, 118, 1–31. [409]

Crawford, Vincent P and Joel Sobel (1982), "Strategic information transmission." *Econometrica*, 50, 1431–1451. [409]

Deneckere, Raymond and Sergei Severinov (2003), "Mechanism design and communication costs." Working paper, Fuqua School of Business, Duke University. [409]

Fishman, Michael J. and Kathleen M. Hagerty (1990), "The optimal amount of discretion to allow in disclosure." *Quarterly Journal of Economics*, 105, 427–444. [409]

Forges, Frangoise and Frédéric Koessler (2005), "Communication equilibria with partially verifiable types." *Journal of Mathematical Economics*, 41, 793–811. [409]

Glazer, Jacob and Ariel Rubinstein (2001), "Debates and decisions: On a rationale of argumentation rules." *Games and Economic Behavior*, 36, 158–173. [396,409]

Glazer, Jacob and Ariel Rubinstein (2004), "On optimal rules of persuasion." *Econometrica*, 72, 1715–1736. [396, 398, 400, 401, 402, 409]

Green, Jerry R. and Jean-Jacques Laffont (1986), "Partially verifiable information and mechanism design." *Review of Economic Studies*, 53, 447–456. [409]

Grice, H. Paul (1989), *Studies in the Way of Words*. Harvard University Press, Cambridge, Mass. [395]

Lipman, Barton L. and Duane J. Seppi (1995), "Robust inference in communication games with partial provability." *Journal of Economic Theory*, 66, 370–405. [409]

Milgrom, Paul and John Roberts (1986), "Relying on the information of interested parties." *Rand Journal of Economics*, 17, 18–32. [409]

Rubinstein, Ariel (2000), *Economics and Language*. Cambridge University Press, Cambridge. [409]

Shin, Hyun Song (1994), "The burden of proof in a game of persuasion." *Journal of Economic Theory*, 64, 253–264. [409]

Townsend, Robert M. (1979), "Optimal contracts and competitive markets with costly state verification." *Journal of Economic Theory*, 21, 265–293. [409]

Chapter 6

A Model of Persuasion with Boundedly Rational Agents

Jacob Glazer

Tel Aviv University and Boston University

Ariel Rubinstein

Tel Aviv University and New York University

A new model of persuasion is presented. A listener first announces and commits
to a codex (i.e., a set of conditions). The speaker then presents a (not
necessarily true) profile that must satisfy the codex in order for the listener to
be persuaded. The speaker is boundedly rational in the sense that his ability
to come up with a persuasive profile is limited and depends on the true profile
and the content and framing of the codex. The circumstances under which the
listener can design a codex that will implement his goal are fully characterized.

1. Introduction

I went to a bar and was told it was full. I asked the bar hostess by what
time one should arrive in order to get in. She said by 12 PM and that once
the bar is full you can only get in if you are meeting a friend who is already
inside. So I lied and said that my friend was already inside. Without having
been told, I would not have known which of the possible lies to tell in order
to get in. (M.R. describing an actual experience at a Tel Aviv bar)

In this episode, M.R. was trying to persuade the bar's hostess to let him
in. The hostess revealed the conditions for her to be persuaded though she
had no way of verifying whether M.R. satisfies those conditions. Thus, her

---

Rubinstein acknowledges financial support from European Research Council grant
269143. We wish to thank Noga Alon, Ayala Arad, Sambuddha Ghosh, Bart Lipman,
Michael Richter, Rani Spiegler, and Jaber Zarezadeh. Our special thanks to Chuck
Wilson for his very useful comments and suggestions, especially regarding proposition 7.

statement also guided M.R. how to lie effectively in order to gain entrance to the bar.

Consider another example: A search committee would like to identify those candidates who exhibit consistency in their preferences, in the sense that when asked to choose between plans of action, their preferences satisfy transitivity. The committee members view a consistency of this form to be a desirable attribute for the job. Therefore, the candidates are given the following test: A hypothetical scenario is described to them that involves three possible plans of actions, denoted as a, b, and c. Each candidate is then asked to answer three questions of the form "Which plan do you prefer, x or y?" The candidate responds to each question by saying either "I prefer x to y" (denoted as $x \succ y$) or "I prefer y to x" (denoted as $y \succ x$). Assume that the committee is required to inform the candidates of the conditions that their answers must fulfill in order to pass the test. Suppose that the committee announces the following set of conditions (hereafter referred to as a *codex*):

R1. If $a \succ b$ and $b \succ c$, then $a \succ c$.
R2. If $b \succ a$ and $c \succ b$, then $c \succ a$.
R3. If $a \succ b$ and $a \succ c$, then $c \succ b$.
R4. If $c \succ a$ and $c \succ b$, then $a \succ b$.

Notice that the codex is satisfied only by the four (transitive) orderings in which b is not positioned in the middle.

If a candidate is fully rational, he can come up with answers to the three questions that satisfy all four conditions and thus pass the test, regardless of what his true preferences are. However, this is no longer the case if the candidate's ability to come up with a set of answers that satisfies the codex is limited and depends on the individual's true preferences, which is the assumption of our analysis.

Consider three candidates named Alice, Bob, and Carol who are all eager to get the job and are willing to lie about their preferences in order to succeed.

Alice holds the ordering $a \succ c \succ b$ and thus satisfies all four conditions. She can pass the test by simply telling the truth.

Bob holds the ordering $a \succ b \succ c$. His ordering does not satisfy the codex since it satisfies the antecedent of R3 but violates R3's consequent. Bob can pass the test by telling the truth about his preferences between a and b and between a and c (thus satisfying the antecedent of R3) and lying about his preferences between b and c (such that the consequent of

R3 is also satisfied). In other words, R3 not only informs Bob that his true preferences will be rejected but also guides him in how to lie in order to pass the test (i.e., by declaring the ordering $a \succ c \succ b$).

Carol holds the cyclical preferences $a \succ b \succ c \succ a$. The only antecedent she satisfies is that of R1; however, she violates R1's consequent. If she uses R1 as a guide in formulating her answers, she will declare the ordering $a \succ b \succ c$ and will fail the test.

In short, all Alice has to do in order to pass the test is tell the truth. Bob and Carol, on the other hand, will fail if they tell the truth. According to our main assumption and given the codex described above, Bob can lie successfully but Carol cannot. The codex guides Bob, who holds an ordering in which b is in the middle, to switch the positions of b and c and thus satisfy the codex. Carol, whose preferences are cyclical, is not guided to an ordering in which b is in last place. Our assumption, presented formally in the next section, is that when faced with such a codex, individuals are able to come up with successful answers if and only if either their true preferences satisfy the codex (as in the case of Alice) or they are guided by the codex to a set of answers that satisfy all the conditions (as in the case of Bob). Under this assumption, only individuals with transitive preferences will be able to pass the test, either by telling the truth or by lying successfully.

The above two scenarios are examples of persuasion situations. A persuasion situation involves a speaker and a listener. The speaker attempts to persuade the listener to take a certain action or to adopt a certain position. The interests of the two parties are not necessarily identical and depend on the speaker's "profile," that is, a set of relevant nonverifiable attributes (or facts) known only to the speaker. The speaker would like the listener to choose his desired action regardless of his true profile, whereas the listener wishes to be persuaded only if the speaker's profile satisfies certain conditions (i.e., belongs to a certain set). In his attempt to persuade the listener, the speaker presents a "profile," which is not necessarily the true one. However, cheating effectively (i.e., presenting a persuasive false profile) may be difficult since it requires the speaker to invent a fictitious profile. The listener is aware of the fact that the speaker may be providing false information that is not verifiable. He is also aware of the procedure used by the speaker to come up with a persuasive false profile.

We model a persuasion situation as a leader-follower relationship. First, the listener (leader) announces and commits to a persuasion rule (a codex), that is, a set of conditions that the profile presented by the speaker must satisfy in order for the listener to be persuaded. Then, the speaker (follower) chooses a profile to present. In order to persuade the listener, the speaker can present a false profile, and this is where bounded rationality is introduced. We assume that the speaker's ability to come up with a persuasive profile is limited and depends on his true profile, the content of the persuasion rule, and the way in which the rule is framed.

Modeling the idea that the speaker's ability to cheat is limited could have been carried out in a framework similar to that of Green and Laffont (1986) (which was also the approach taken in Glazer and Rubinstein [2004, 2006]). In this type of model, the set of messages that the speaker had to choose from is exogenously given and dependent on the speaker's profile. The novelty of the current paper lies in the assumption that not only is cheating difficult but also the speaker's ability to cheat effectively depends on the way in which the persuasion rule is framed. In such a case, the desirable persuasion rule should be complex enough that a speaker whose profile should not be persuasive will not be able to persuade the listener by manipulating the information but, at the same time, should be simple enough that a speaker whose profile should be persuasive will indeed be able to persuade the listener.

The reader may wonder under what circumstances mechanisms of the type discussed in this paper will be relevant. We have in mind situations such as the following: a patient trying to persuade a doctor to prescribe him a particular treatment, a parent trying to persuade a school committee to transfer her child to another school, a taxpayer trying to persuade the tax authorities that he has paid the right amount of tax, a crime suspect trying to persuade his interrogators to set him free, and so on. In such situations, an agent is required (by the principal) to answer some questions about facts he knows. The answers to the questions (or at least to some of them) are not (easily) verifiable by the principal, and the agent's objective is to come up with answers — not necessarily true ones — that will "persuade" the principal. The time available to the agent for coming up with persuasive answers (or his ability to do so) is limited, and he does not have access to expert advice. In such cases, the agent will use some simple (and not necessarily fully rational) procedure in order to provide convincing answers. It is reasonable to assume that the truth will play a major role in such a procedure. If the principal is familiar with the speaker's procedure, he may be able to design the questions in such a way that only the requests of agents that should be accepted by the principal will indeed be accepted.

In what follows, we introduce our new approach to modeling bounded rationality. After presenting the model we define and explore two notions of implementation. The listener's goal is "implementable" if there exists a codex that enables the speaker to persuade the listener (either by telling the truth or by cheating) if and only if the listener would want the speaker's true profile to be persuasive. The listener's goal is "truthfully implementable" if it is implementable and any speaker who is able to persuade the listener can do so without lying. The main body of the analysis consists of a full characterization of the conditions under which the listener's goal is implementable and the conditions under which the listener's goal is truthfully implementable.

2. The Model

The Set of Profiles

Let V be a set of $K \geq 2$ propositional variables denoted by $v_1, \ldots, v_K$. Each variable can take one of two truth values: "*T*rue" or "*F*alse." A *profile* is a truth assignment for each of the variables. Denote by $s(v)$ the truth value of the variable v in the profile s. We will sometimes present a profile s as a K-vector $(s_1, \ldots, s_K)$ of 0s and 1s, where $s_k = 1$ means that $s(v_k) = T$ and $s_k = 0$ means that $s(v_k) = F$.

Let S be the set of all profiles. We assume that all 2^K profiles are logically possible, namely, that the content of the variables is such that the truth combination of some of the variables does not exclude the truth combination of any of the others as would have been the case, for example, if v_1 was "being a female" and v_2 was "being a male."

The Speaker and the Listener

There are two agents: a speaker and a listener. The speaker knows which profile is true whereas the listener knows only the set S. The speaker wishes to persuade the listener to accept a particular request regardless of the true profile. The listener can either accept or reject the request. He would like to accept the speaker's request only if the profile belongs to a given set A. Let $R = S - A$ be the set of profiles for which the listener would like to reject the speaker's request.

We analyze the following leader-follower scenario: First, the listener announces and commits to a codex, which is a set of conditions that the profile presented by the speaker must satisfy in order for the speaker's request to be accepted. Then, the speaker (who knows the true profile) announces a profile that may or may not be the true one. The listener is committed to applying the codex to the profile announced by the speaker.

Comment. — As stated above, we do not consider situations in which some profiles in S are "impossible." Doing so would require specifying whether the speaker knows which profiles are impossible. If the speaker does not know which profiles are impossible, then the listener's task becomes easier. There are two reasons for this: the listener will have less "undeserving" profiles to worry about and in some cases he can expose an undeserving speaker by guiding him to declare an impossible profile.

The Codex

A *codex* is defined as a set of propositions in propositional logic that uses only the variables in the set V. A proposition in the codex is referred to as a *rule*. Only a profile that does not violate any of the propositions will "persuade" the listener. We impose two restrictions on a codex:

1. *Structure*: Each rule φ in the codex must have the structure $\wedge_{y \in W} \varphi_y \rightarrow \varphi_x$, where W is a nonempty subset of $V, x \in V - W$, and each φ_v is either v or $-v$ (the negation of v). For example, the proposition $v_4 \wedge -v_1 \rightarrow v_3$ can be a rule in a codex but $v_1 \rightarrow -v_1$ cannot. For any given rule $\varphi = \wedge_{y \in I} \varphi_y \rightarrow \varphi_x$, we denote $a(\varphi) = \wedge_{y \in I} \varphi_y$ (the antecedent of φ) and $z(\varphi) = \varphi_x$ (the consequent of φ). We interpret a rule as a statement of the following form made by the listener: "If your profile satisfies the antecedent of the rule, then it should also satisfy the consequent."

2. *Coherence*: The codex cannot contain rules that conflict in the sense that there is no pair of rules such that their antecedents do not conflict and their consequents do (one consequent is v and the other is $-v$ for the same variable v). Formally, a codex is coherent if it does not contain two rules $\varphi = \wedge_{y \in W_1} \varphi_y \rightarrow x$ and $\psi = \wedge_{y \in W_2} \psi_y \rightarrow -x$, where for any $y \in W_1 \cap W_2$ we have $\varphi_y = \psi_y$. Thus, coherence does not only require that a codex not contain the two rules $v_1 \rightarrow v_2$ and $v_1 \rightarrow -v_2$ but also that it will not contain the two rules $v_1 \rightarrow v_3$ and $v_2 \rightarrow -v_3$ (i.e., the antecedents do not conflict but the consequents do). In our view, a codex containing these two rules is problematic: a speaker whose true profile, s, is such that $s(v_1) = s(v_2) = T$ will rightly complain that the codex imposes two conflicting requirements on him with regard to the variable v_3.

To illustrate, in the second example that appeared in the introduction, the three variables are $v_1 = a \succ b$, $v_2 = b \succ c$, and $v_3 = c \succ a$, and the proposed codex consists of the following four rules: $v_1 \wedge v_2 \rightarrow -v_3$, $-v_1 \wedge -v_2 \rightarrow v_3$, $v_1 \wedge -v_3 \rightarrow -v_2$, and $v_3 \wedge -v_2 \rightarrow v_1$.

Given a codex Λ, let $T(\Lambda)$ be the set of profiles that satisfy all propositions in Λ. In other words, $T(\Lambda)$ is the set of profiles that, if announced by the speaker, will persuade the listener. More precisely, using the notation $s \models \psi$ for "proposition ψ is true in profile s," $T(\Lambda) = \{s|s \models \varphi$ for all $\varphi \in \Lambda\}$.

Recall that $s \models \Lambda_{y \in I} \psi_y \rightarrow \psi_x$ unless (i) the antecedent of ψ is satisfied; that is, for all $y \in I$ we have $s(y) = T$ if $\psi_y = y$ and $s(y) = F$ if $\psi_y = -y$; and (ii) the consequent of ψ is violated; that is, either $s(x) = T$ and $\psi_x = -x$ or $s(x) = F$ and $\psi_x = x$.

The Speaker's Choice Procedure

The speaker can either state the true profile or make up a false one. A fully rational speaker can come up with a profile that satisfies the codex regardless of what the true profile is. We assume, however, that the speaker is boundedly rational in the sense that he is limited in his ability to come up with a persuasive false profile. Essentially we assume that the speaker applies the following procedure (a formal discussion will follow).

Step 1. Determine whether your true profile satisfies the codex.

  If it does, then announce the true profile. If it does not, then go to step 2.

Step 2. Find a rule (not considered in a previous round of step 2) that is violated by your true profile (i.e., your true profile satisfies the rule's antecedent but violates its consequent). Change the truth value of the variable that appears in the consequent of this rule and determine whether the modified profile satisfies the codex.

  If it does, announce the new profile. If it does not, iterate step 2.

Step 3. If you are unable to come up with a modified profile that satisfies the codex in step 2, announce your true profile.

Guidance

We say that, given Λ, the speaker is guided to s' from s (denoted as $s \rightarrow_\Lambda s'$) if for every variable v for which $s'(v) \neq s(v)$, there is a rule $\varphi \in \Lambda$ such that (1) $s \models a(\varphi)$ and $s' \models a(\varphi)$ and (2) $s' \models z(\varphi)$ (i.e., if $z(\varphi) = v$, then $s'(v) = T$, and if $z(\varphi) = -v$, then $s'(v) = F$). In other words, the speaker is guided from s to s' if any switch from $s(v)$ to $s'(v)$ is triggered by a rule that requires that the value of the variable v will be $s'(v)$ and its antecedent is satisfied at s and refers only to the variables that are kept unchanged. We refer to the relation $\rightarrow_\Lambda$ as the guidance relation induced by Λ.

The speaker may be guided from one profile to several others. For example, suppose that $K = 4$ and Λ contains the three rules $v \rightarrow -v_3$, $v_2 \rightarrow -v_4$, and $v_2 \wedge v_3 \wedge v_4 \rightarrow -v_1$. Then, the speaker is guided by Λ from $(1, 1, 1, 1)$ to each of the profiles $(1, 1, 1, 1)$, $(1, 1, 0, 1)$, $(1, 1, 1, 0)$, $(1, 1, 0, 0)$, and $(0, 1, 1, 1)$.

Persuasion

Given a codex Λ, we say that the speaker whose profile is s can persuade the listener if $s \rightarrow_\Lambda s'$ for some $s' \in T(\Lambda)$. Define $P(\Lambda) = \{s | s \rightarrow_\Lambda s'$ for some $s' \in T(\Lambda)\}$. That is, $P(\Lambda)$ is the set of profiles for which the speaker can persuade the listener. Obviously $T(\Lambda) \subseteq P(\Lambda)$. Note that it is possible for the speaker to be guided from the true profile to profiles that are persuasive and others that are not. By our definition, the speaker is able to persuade the listener if he is guided to at least one persuasive profile. Note also that we do not allow the speaker to be guided sequentially, that is, first from s to s' and then from s' to s''. Later on, we will comment on these two assumptions.

Implementation

The set A is implementable if there is a codex Λ such that $P(\Lambda) = A$. The set A is truthfully implementable if there is a codex Λ such that $T(\Lambda) = P(\Lambda) = A$.

Thus, if a codex implements A, then the speaker is able to persuade the listener in all profiles for which the listener should be persuaded and in none of the profiles for which he should not. However, in some of the cases in which the listener should be persuaded, the speaker has to "alter the truth" in order to persuade the listener. If a codex truthfully implements A, then a speaker whose profile should persuade the listener is able to do so by simply telling the truth.

Note that the "revelation principle" does not hold in our framework, and as we will see later, there are cases in which the set A is implementable but not truthfully implementable.

Comment. — The following analogy may help clarify our concept of implementation. Suppose that you manage a large network of agents around the globe. The location of each agent is characterized by two coordinates. Suppose that you want to award a prize only to those agents whose locations are in the set A. You do not know who is located where, but you do know that all agents use the same program to solve systems of equations. Whether the program will converge to a solution depends on the system and the initial conditions inserted into the program. You also know that people tend to input their true coordinates as the initial conditions. In such a case, you can try to come up with a system of equations such that the program will converge to a solution within a specified time if and only if it starts from a point in the set A. If you can find such a system of equations, it will serve as a mechanism for selecting the agents that you want to award. Note that a rule in our model is actually an equation in which the propositional variables are the unknowns while a codex is in fact a system of equations.

The assumptions regarding the structure of the codex, as well as the speaker's choice procedure when facing such a codex, are to some extent arbitrary. Nevertheless, we believe that they capture some realistic and important elements common to many persuasion situations. The structure of the codex resembles that of many legal codes, and the speaker's decision procedure captures procedural elements observed in the behavior of people in response to such codes. In what follows, we discuss the generality of some of our assumptions in more detail.

Structure of the codex. — Our codex does not allow for rules in which the consequent is a conjunction, such as $v_1 \wedge v_2 \rightarrow v_3 \wedge v_4$. However, note that this rule is logically equivalent to the two rules $v_1 \wedge v_2 \rightarrow v_3$ and $v_1 \wedge v_2 \rightarrow v_4$, which our codex does allow. Similarly, rules with a disjunction in their consequent, such as $v_1 \wedge v_2 \rightarrow v_3 \vee v_4$, can be expressed in our codex by the two rules $v_1 \wedge v_2 \wedge -v_3 \rightarrow v_4$ and $v_1 \wedge v_2 \wedge -v_4 \rightarrow v_3$. Neither do we allow the codex to have rules without any consequent, such as $v_1 \wedge v_2$ (formally, this is a rule with an empty antecedent), since such a rule would provide the speaker (regardless of his true profile) with all the information he needs to make a persuasive declaration with respect to the variables v_1 and v_2 (recall the example of M.R. in the introduction). Disjunctions, such as $v_1 \vee v_2$, can be represented in our codex by pairs of rules such as $-v_1 \rightarrow v_2$ and $-v_2 \rightarrow v_1$.

Coherence. — It will become clear below that eliminating the requirement that a codex be coherent will make the listener's job much easier (more sets will then be implementable). However, incoherent codexes are unintuitive and unrealistic. We interpret rules of the type $v_1 \wedge v_2 \rightarrow -v_3$ as a declaration by the listener that "if your profile satisfies v_1 and v_2, then it must not satisfy v_3." Under such an interpretation, a noncoherent codex would require an individual to have and, at the same time, not to have a particular characteristic, a feature that is unacceptable.

The speaker's choice procedure. — The main feature of the speaker's choice procedure is that the speaker starts from the true profile (rather than from another prominent profile, such as, e.g., the "all-truth" profile) and moves from that profile in a "direction" suggested to him by the codex. If that direction leads to an acceptable profile, it is assumed that the speaker returns to the true profile and tries another direction. Note that if the speaker's behavior is completely independent of the true profile, then the listener is unable to learn what he would like to about the speaker's true profile.

An alternative assumption would be that the speaker does not return to his true profile when he encounters a rule that his new profile violates. Rather he changes direction, as suggested by the codex, and relates to the new profile as if it were the truth. Implementation under this procedure (to be referred to as "iterative guidance") will be examined in proposition 4.

In this paper we do not explore the many other possible procedures that the speaker could adopt, such as modifying his profile in order to violate the antecedent rather than to satisfy the consequent of a rule that his profile violates.

The results of experiments we conducted (see Sec. VII) support the key features of the procedure studied in this paper. Nonetheless, we do not claim that the procedure precisely describes behavior in such circumstances. The model should be viewed more as a prototype for implementation models, in which the designer takes into account the bounded rationality of the agents.

3. Examples

Example 1. Assume that there are three "scenarios," numbered 1, 2, and 3, and an individual's attitude toward each one can be either "positive" or "negative." A principal would like to identify those individuals who are consistent in their attitude toward the three scenarios, that is, who have the same attitude toward all three. In order to do so, the principal performs the following test: each individual is asked to state his attitude (positive or negative) toward each of the three scenarios. Let the variable v_i, stand for "the individual's attitude toward scenario i is positive" and therefore $A = \{(1,1,1),(0,0,0)\}$. Consider the following three codexes.

Λ_1: "The second and third answers should be the same as the first" ($\Lambda_1 = \{v_1 \rightarrow v_2, -v \rightarrow -v_2, v_1 \rightarrow v_3, -v_1 \rightarrow -v_3\}$). In this case, $T(\Lambda_1) = A$ and $P(\Lambda_1) = S$ since for any profile (s_1, s_2, s_3) we have $(s_1, s_2, s_3) \rightarrow_{\Lambda_1} (s_1, s_1, s_1) \in T(\Lambda_1)$.

Λ_2: "The second answer should be the same as the first and the third answer should be the same as the second" ($\Lambda_2 = \{v_1 \rightarrow v_2, -v_1 \rightarrow -v_2, v_2 \rightarrow v_3, -v_2 \rightarrow -v_3\}$). In this case, $T(\Lambda_2) = A$ but $P(\Lambda_2) = S - \{(1,0,0), (0,1,1)\}$ (since $(1,0,0)$ is guided only to $(1,1,0)$).

Λ_3: The three scenarios are ordered clockwise. For every scenario i the codex requires that if the answer regarding scenario i is different from the answer regarding scenario $i+1$ (which follows i), then the answer regarding scenario $i+2$ should coincide with the answer regarding scenario $i+1$. (The codex Λ_3 contains the three rules $-v_i \wedge v_{i+1} \rightarrow v_{i+2}$ [for all i] and the three rules $v_i \wedge -v_{i+1} \rightarrow -v_{i+2}$ [for all i].)

Codex Λ_3 truthfully implements A since $P(\Lambda_3) = T(\Lambda_3) = A$. Thus, although the three codexes are satisfied by the same set of profiles, only the third codex implements the principal's goal.

Example 2. A principal would like to select "decisive" individuals (regardless of the opinions they hold) for a particular task. In order to do so he presents the candidates with a dilemma and three possible exclusive solutions (denoted by 1, 2, and 3). He then asks each candidate whether each of the three possible solutions is appropriate. The principal wishes to identify those individuals who view exactly one solution to be appropriate (regardless of which one it is). Let v_i stand for "solution i is appropriate" and therefore $A = \{(1,0,0),(0,1,0),(0,0,1)\}$.

We will show that A is not implementable. Assume that Λ implements A.

Case 1: $T(\Lambda) = A$. The profile $(0,0,0)$ is not in $T(\Lambda)$, and hence there is a rule in Λ that this profile violates; without loss of generality (w.l.o.g.), that rule is either $-v_1 \rightarrow v_3$ or $-v_1 \wedge -v_2 \rightarrow v_3$. In both cases $(0,0,0) \rightarrow_\Lambda (0,0,1)$ and hence $(0,0,0) \in P(\Lambda)$, although $(0,0,0) \notin A$, a contradiction.

Case 2: One of the profiles in A, w.l.o.g. $(0,0,1)$, is not in $T(\Lambda)$. Then, there must be another profile in A, w.l.o.g. $(0,1,0)$, such that $(0,0,1) \rightarrow_\Lambda$

$(0,1,0)$. This requires that $-v_1 \rightarrow v_2$ be in the codex. However, in that case, $(0,0,0) \rightarrow_\Lambda (0,1,0) \in T(\Lambda)$ and therefore $(0,0,0) \in P(\Lambda)$ although $(0,0,0) \notin A$, a contradiction.

Note that even though the above set is not implementable its complement is. Let $A' = S - A$. Consider the codex Λ' that consists of the three rules $v_i \rightarrow v_j$, where $j \neq i + 1$ ("3 + 1" is taken to be "1"). Obviously, $T(\Lambda') = \{\text{all } F, \text{all } T\}$. The codex guides the speaker to "all T" from every profile in R' except for "all F." For any $s \in R'$ where there is a unique v_i, for which $s(v_i) = T$, the speaker is guided from s only to profiles for which v_{i+1} receives the value F and hence violates the codex. Thus, $s \notin P(\Lambda')$.

Example 3. A certain individual (the listener) holds a positive opinion on K issues. He would like to find out whether another individual (the speaker) shares his opinion on at least m of those issues, where $0 < m < K$. Let $A_m = \{s | s \text{ receives the value } T \text{ for at least } m \text{ variables}\}$, where $0 < m < K$. We will show that A_m is implementable.

Let Λ be the codex that consists of all rules $R(y, W)$ (where y is a variable and W is a set of at most m variables that does not contain y), which states that if the variables in W receive the value T and the variables in $V - W - \{y\}$ receive the value F, then y should also get the value T. (Formally, $R(y, W) = [\wedge_{v \in W} v] \wedge [\wedge_{v \in X - W - \{y\}} -v] \rightarrow y$.) Obviously, $T(\Lambda) = A_{m+1}$ and $P(\Lambda) = A_m$. Thus, the speaker whose profile assigns the truth value T to up to m variables is guided to "slightly exaggerate" and to claim that there is one more variable that receives the value T. This codex will not guide speakers whose profiles have less than m true variables to cheat effectively. In this case, the implementation is not truthful, but as will be shown later in proposition 3, A_m is in fact truthfully implementable for $K > 3$ and $m > 2$.

4. Auxiliary Concepts and Results

Before characterizing the implementable sets, we need to introduce some auxiliary concepts and results.

Properties of the Relation $\rightarrow_\Lambda$

Lemma 1.

a. *The relation $\rightarrow_\Lambda$ is reflexive and antisymmetric (i.e., for any two distinct profiles s and s', if $s \rightarrow_\Lambda s'$, then $s' \not\rightarrow_\Lambda s$).*
b. *If s is opposed to $s'(s(v) \neq s'(v)$ for all $v)$, then $s \not\rightarrow_\Lambda s'$.*

c. *If $s \rightarrow_\Lambda t$ and s' is between s and t (i.e., $s(v) \neq s'(v)$ implies that $s'(v) = t(v)$), then $s \rightarrow_\Lambda s'$ and $s' \rightarrow_\Lambda t$.*

Proof. Antisymmetry follows from the assumption that the codex is coherent. The rest of the lemma follows immediately from the definition of the relation $\rightarrow_\Lambda$. $\square$

The next lemma shows that the guidance relation $\rightarrow_\Lambda$ fully conveys the information about $T(\Lambda)$, the set of profiles that satisfy the codex Λ. Given a binary relation $\rightarrow$, denote $T(\rightarrow) = \{s \mid$ for no $t \neq s, s \rightarrow t\}$ and $P(\rightarrow) = \{s \mid$ there is $t \in T(\rightarrow)$ such that $s \rightarrow t\}$.

Lemma 2.

a. $T(\Lambda) = T(\rightarrow_\Lambda)$.
b. $P(\Lambda) = P(\rightarrow_\Lambda)$.

Proof. Part a: Assume that $s \notin T(\Lambda)$. Then there is a rule $\varphi = \wedge_{y \in I}\varphi_y \rightarrow \varphi_x$ in Λ such that $s \models \varphi$ is not true; that is, s satisfies the antecedent $\wedge_{y \in I}\varphi_y$ but not the consequent φ_x. Thus, $s \rightarrow_\Lambda s'$ where s' is the profile that differs from s only in the truth value of the variable x, that is, $s \notin T(\rightarrow_\Lambda)$.

In the other direction, assume that $s \notin T(\rightarrow_\Lambda)$. Then there is a profile $t \neq s$ such that $s \rightarrow_\Lambda t$. Thus, there is a variable x and a rule $\varphi = \wedge_{y \in I}\varphi_y \rightarrow \varphi_x$ such that s and t satisfy φ's antecedent, $t(x) \neq s(x)$, and $t \models \varphi$. Hence, s does not satisfy φ, and therefore, $s \notin T(\Lambda)$.

Part b: The proof follows from part a and the definitions $P(\Lambda) = \{s \mid s \rightarrow_\Lambda s'$ for some $s' \in T(\Lambda)\}$ and $P(\rightarrow_\Lambda) = \{s \mid s \rightarrow_\Lambda s'$ for some $s' \in T(\rightarrow_\Lambda)\}$. $\square$

The Neighborhood Relation

A key element in the analysis is the neighborhood binary relation N on the set S. Define sNs' to mean that s and s' differ in the truth value of exactly one variable. The relation N is symmetric and irreflexive. Define a distance function $d(s, s') = |\{v \mid s(v) \neq s'(v)\}|$.

A *path* is a sequence of distinct profiles $(s_1, \ldots, s_L)$ such that $s_1 N s_2 N \cdots N s_L$. If $L > 2$ and $s_L N s_1$, then the path is a *cycle*. Any cycle must contain an even number of profiles. We say that a cycle is a *counting cycle* (referred to in graph theory as a Hamiltonian cycle) of the set X if it contains all elements of X. Obviously, S has a counting cycle. A sequence $(s^0, s^1, \ldots, s^L)$ is a *ray* from s^0 if $s^{l+1} N s^l$ and $d(s^l, s^0) = l$.

Let $N(s)$ be the set of neighbors of s. If sNs', then $N(s) \cap N(s') = \varnothing$. For any two profiles s and s', $|N(s) \cap N(s')|$ is either 0 or 2. In particular, if $rNsNt$, then there is a unique u such that (r, s, t, u) is a cycle. Denote this u by $N(r, s, t)$.

Complete Rules

A *complete rule* is a proposition of the type $\wedge_{v \in V - \{x\}} \varphi_v \to \varphi_x$. In other words, its antecedent refers to $K \to 1$ variables and the consequent to the remaining one. If a codex Λ contains the complete rule $\wedge_{v \in V - \{x\}} \varphi_v \to \varphi_x$, then $s \to_\Lambda s'$ where s and s' are the two neighbors defined by $s \models \wedge_{v \in V - \{x\}} \varphi_v \wedge \neg\varphi_x$ and $s' \models \wedge_{v \in V - \{x\}} \varphi_v \wedge \varphi_x$.

For any two neighbors s and s', let $\varphi(s, s')$ be the complete rule $\varphi = \wedge_{v \in V - \{x\}} \varphi_v \wedge \varphi_x$. Thus, $s \to_\Lambda s'$ for any codex Λ that contains φ.

The last lemma in this section demonstrates that the language we use for codexes does not limit the sets that can be specified; that is, it allows the specification of any subset $X \subseteq S$.

Lemma 3. *For every set $X \subseteq S$, there is a codex Λ such that $T(\Lambda) = X$.*

Proof. Let $(s^1, \ldots, s^L)$ be a counting cycle of S. The set $\Lambda = \{\varphi(s^l, s^{l+1}) \mid s^l \notin X\}$ is coherent and thus Λ is a codex. Obviously, $T(\Lambda) = X$. $\square$

A Canonical Codex

A particular type of codex, to be termed canonical, will play a central role in our analysis. A codex is *canonical* if (i) it consists of complete rules; (ii) for every s, there is at most one $t \neq s$ such that $s \to_\Lambda t$; and (iii) for every $s \in P(\Lambda) \to T(\Lambda)$, there is $r \in S - P(\Lambda)$ such that $r \to_\Lambda s$.

Thus, a canonical codex that implements the set A is a set of complete rules such that (a) for every profile $r \in R$ the codex contains a unique rule that is violated by r and (b) a profile $s \in A$ violates the codex only if the codex contains a rule that is violated by some $r \in R$ and guides the speaker to s.

A canonical codex is analytically simple, although it does not necessarily have a natural interpretation. If it implements the set A, then the number of rules it contains is at least equal to the number of profiles in R and thus can be very large. A canonical codex makes the speaker's task relatively simple since by condition ii it guides the speaker to at most one alternative profile. Condition iii is relevant only in the case of nontruthful implementation, and it requires that a profile in A not be rejected by the codex unless the listener uses that particular profile to "deal" with some other profiles in R that the listener would like to block.

5. Truthful Implementation

In this section, we fully characterize the truthfully implementable sets. In particular, we show that when a set A is truthfully implementable, implementation can be achieved by a canonical codex that consists of $|R|$ complete rules, each of which guides a distinct profile s in R to a neighboring profile in R.

Proposition 1. *If the set A is truthfully implementable, then it is truthfully implementable by a canonical codex.*

Proof. Let Λ be a codex such that $T(\Lambda) = P(\Lambda) = A$. By Lemma 2, $T(\Lambda) = T(\rightarrow_\Lambda)$, and thus for every $s \in R$ there is a profile $t \neq s$ such that $s \rightarrow_\Lambda t$. Let $n(s)$ be some neighbor of s that is between s and t. By Lemma 1, we have $s \rightarrow_\Lambda n(s) \rightarrow_\Lambda t$ and therefore $n(s) \notin T(\Lambda)$. The canonical codex $\Lambda' = \{\varphi(s, n(s)) \mid s \in R\}$ truthfully implements A. $\square$

We say that a set of profiles C is *connected* if for any two profiles s, $s' \in C$ there is a path of elements in C connecting s and s'. The set C is a connected component of R if it is a maximal connected subset of R.

The next proposition states that a set A is truthfully implementable if and only if the set R is a union of connected components, each of which contains a cycle. Truthful implementation is accomplished by means of a codex that traps all "undeserving" speakers (i.e., speakers whose profile should not be accepted) in a "circle of lies." In other words, an undeserving speaker is (mis)guided by the codex to pretend to be a neighboring undeserving speaker whose profile is rejected by the codex and who, in turn, is guided by the codex to pretend to be a third neighboring undeserving speaker whose profile is rejected and so on. Eventually this chain creates a cycle.

Proposition 2. *The set A is truthfully implementable if and only if every connected component of R contains a cycle.*

Proof. Assume that A is truthfully implementable. By Proposition 1, the set is implementable by a canonical codex Λ. Then, for every $s \in R$ there is a unique profile $n(s) \in R$ such that $sNn(s)$ and $s \rightarrow_\Lambda n(s)$. Let s_1 be an arbitrary profile in R. Define $s_{l+1} = n(s_l)$. By the finiteness of R we have $s_L = s_{L'}$ for some $L' < L$. Thus, s_1 is connected in R to a cycle in R.

In the other direction, assume that any connected component of R has a cycle. Define the binary relation $\rightarrow$ on R as follows: Let C be a connected component of R. Select a subset of profiles in C that form a cycle $s_1 N s_2 N \cdots N s_L N s_1$. For any l, add $s_l \rightarrow s_{l+1}$ to the relation ($L + 1$ is taken to be 1). For any element $s \in C - \{s_1, \ldots, s_L\}$, choose one of the shortest paths $t_1 N t_2 \cdots N t_N$ of profiles in C where $t_1 = s$ and t_N is in the cycle and add $t_1 \rightarrow t_2$ to the relation. Let $\Lambda = \{\varphi(s, s') \mid s \rightarrow s'\}$. Obviously, the relation $\rightarrow$ is antisymmetric, and thus Λ is coherent. The relation $\rightarrow_\Lambda$ is identical to $\rightarrow$ and $P(\Lambda) = T(\Lambda) = A$. $\qquad\square$

The following proposition describes families of sets that are truthfully implementable. The first family consists of all sets that are "small" in the sense that they contain no more than $K - 1$ profiles. Each of the sets in the second family consists of all profiles for which the number of variables that are true exceeds a certain threshold. The sets belonging to the third family have the property that a particular variable is true (or false) for all profiles included in the set. The fourth family consists of all sets for which there are two variables, such that the inclusion of a profile in the set is independent of their truth values. These two "degenerate" variables are used in the codex merely to "confuse" the undeserving speaker.

Proposition 3. *For $K \geq 3$, any set A that satisfies at least one of the following conditions is truthfully implementable:*

1. *A is "small" with at most $K - 1$ profiles.*
2. *The number of true variables must exceed a threshold: there exists a number $m \geq 3$ such that $A = A_m = \{s \mid$ at least m variables receive the value T at $s\}$.*
3. *There is a particular variable whose value must be true (or false): there exists a variable v such that $A \subseteq T(v)$ (or $T(-v)$), where $T(v)$ is the set of all profiles in which v receives the value T.*
4. *There are two irrelevant variables v' and v'' such that if $s \in A$, then so is any profile s' for which $s(v) = s'(v)$ for all v other than v' and v''.*

Proof. By proposition 2, it is sufficient to show that every $s \in R$ is connected by a path in R to a cycle in R.

Part 1: First, we show that the set R is connected. It is well known that for any two profiles s and t in R that are not neighbors, there are K "disjoint" paths connecting s and t. Since A contains at most $K-1$ elements, at least one of the paths contains only elements of R. Thus, R is connected.

Second, we show that R contains a cycle. Otherwise, let $s_1 N s_2 N \cdots N s_L$ be a longest path of distinct elements in R. Since R contains more than half of the profiles, there must be two opposing profiles belonging to R and thus $L \geq K+1 \geq 4$.

Since $s_3 \in N(s_2) \cap N(s_4)$, there is another profile x such that $s_2 N x N s_4$. The profile x must be in A since otherwise (s_2, s_3, s_4, x) forms a cycle in R. The profile x is not a neighbor of s_1 since s_1 is a neighbor of s_2. The set $N(s_1)$ consists of $s_2 \in R$ and $K-1$ other profiles. It is impossible that all of them are in A since x is not one of them. Thus, $N(s_1)$ contains another element in R (in addition to s_2) and we can extend the path.

Part 2: The set R is connected since each profile in R is connected to the "all F" profile. The set R contains the $2K$-element cycle: $((1,0,\ldots,0),\ (1,1,0,\ldots,0),\ (0,1,0,\ldots,0),\ (0,1,1,0,\ldots,0),\ldots,$ $(0,0,\ldots,1),\ (1,0,\ldots,0,1))$.

Part 3: Since $A \subseteq T(v)$, the set $T(-v) \subseteq R$ and it has a counting cycle. Any element in R either is in $T(-v)$ or is a neighbor of a profile in $T(-v)$. Thus, R is connected and contains a cycle.

Part 4: Any $s \in R$ belongs to a cycle consisting of the four profiles in the set $\{t \mid t(v) = s(v) \text{ for any } v \notin \{v', v''\}\}$. By assumption these four profiles are in R. □

An alternative interpretation of truthful implementation. — Let $K = 3$ and let $\Lambda = \{v_1 \to v_2, v_2 \to v_3\}$. Then $(1,0,0) \to_\Lambda (1,1,0)$ and $(1,1,0) \to_A$ $(1,1,1)$. However, by our assumptions, the speaker is not guided iteratively and thus is not guided from $(1,0,0)$ to the persuasive profile $(1,1,1)$. Had we allowed the speaker to be guided iteratively, the following alternative definition of implementation would have applied.

Definition. We say that A is *implementable in the alternative sense* if there exists a codex Λ such that:

i. for every $s \in A$ there is a chain $s = s_1 \to_\Lambda s_2 \cdots \to_\Lambda s_L$ where $s_L \in T(\Lambda)$;

ii. for no $s \in R$ does there exist a chain $s = s_1 \to_\Lambda s_2 \cdots \to_\Lambda s_L$ where $s_L \in T(\Lambda)$.

Proposition 4. *The set A is implementable in the alternative sense if and only if it is truthfully implementable.*

Proof. If A is truthfully implementable, then the canonical codex built in the proof of Proposition 2 implements A in the alternative sense.

On the other hand, assume that Λ implements the set A in the alternative sense. By condition ii, there is no member of R in $T(\Lambda)$, and thus by Lemma 2 for any $s \in R$ there exists some s' such that $s \to_\Lambda s'$, and by Lemma 3 we can assume w.l.o.g. that $s'Ns$. Had s' been in A, then by condition i there would have been a chain $s' = s_1 \to_\Lambda s_2 \cdots \to_\Lambda s_L$ with $s_L \in T(\Lambda)$, and then we would have had $s' \to_\Lambda s_1 \to_\Lambda s_2 \cdots \to_\Lambda s_L$, contradicting condition ii. Thus, $s' \in R$. Consider the codex $\Lambda' = \{\varphi(s, s') \mid s \in R\}$. Then $P(\Lambda') = T(\Lambda') = A$. □

6. Implementation (Not Necessarily Truthful)

The two main goals of this section are to show that implementation can be achieved by using a canonical codex (Proposition 6) and to characterize the class of implementable sets (Proposition 7). We start with an auxiliary claim.

Proposition 5. *A set A is implementable by a canonical codex if and only if there is a reflexive binary relation $\to$ satisfying the following properties*:

1. *Antisymmetry.*
2. $P(\to) = A$.
3. *If $s \to s'$ and $s \neq s'$, then sNs'.*
4. *For every s there is at most one s' such that $s \to s'$.*
5. *For every $s \in P(\to) - T(\to)$, there is $t \in R$ such that $t \to s$.*

Proof. Assume that A is implementable by a canonical codex Λ. The relation $\to_\Lambda$ satisfies properties 1, 2, 3, 4, and 5 since the coherence of the codex implies property 1, the implementability of A by the codex is equivalent to property 2, and the fact that the codex is canonical implies properties 3, 4, and 5.

On the other hand, given a relation $\to$ that satisfies properties 1, 2, 3, 4, and 5, consider $\Lambda = \{\varphi(s, s') \mid s \neq s' \text{ and } s \to s'\}$. Property 1 implies that the codex is coherent. The relation $\to_\Lambda$ is equal to $\to$, and using property 2 we have $P(\Lambda) = P(\to_\Lambda) = P(\to) = A$. Properties 3, 4, and 5 imply that the codex is canonical. □

Proposition 6. *If the set A is implementable, then it is implementable by a canonical codex.*

Proof.   Let Λ be a codex that implements A. We start with the relation $\to_\Lambda$ and modify it to become a relation satisfying the five properties in Proposition 5.

The relation $\to_\Lambda$ is reflexive, satisfies properties 1 and 2, and in addition has the following property:

6. *Betweenness*: If $s \to_\Lambda s'$ and t is a profile "between" s and s', then $s \to_\Lambda t \to_\Lambda s'$.

First, define a new reflexive relation $\to$ as follows.

a. For every $s \in A - T(\Lambda)$, choose one profile $s' \in T(\Lambda)$ such that $s \to_\Lambda s'$ and define $s \to s'$.
b. For every $s \in R$, choose one profile $s' \neq s$ for which $s \to_\Lambda s'$. Since $\to_\Lambda$ satisfies property 6, we can assume that $s'Ns$. Since $s \notin P(\Lambda)$, $s' \notin T(\Lambda)$. Define $s \to s'$.

The relation $\to$ satisfies properties 1, 2, and 4 as well as the following properties:

7. If $s \in R$, then there is a unique s' such that $s \to s'$ and $s' \notin T(\to)$ and $s'Ns$. If $s \in A$ and $s \to s'$, then $s' \in T(\to)$ and all profiles between s and s' are in A.

We now modify the relation $\to$ recursively as follows:

i. For every $s \in A - T(\to)$ such that the set $N(s) \cap T(\to) \neq \varnothing$ and $s \to x$ for $x \notin N(s)$, divert the relation from $s \to x$ to $s \to y$ for some $y \in N(s) \cap T(\to)$.
ii. Let $s \in A$ be such that $s \to s'$ and $s' \notin N(s)$. Let s'' be a neighbor of s between s and s'. By property 7, $s'' \in A$, and by property 2 there exists $s''' \in T(\to)$ such that $s'' \to s'''$. Delete $s'' \to s'''$ and $s \to s'$ from the relation and add $s \to s''$. If there is a profile $r \to s''$, then $r \in R$ and, by property 7, s'' and r are neighbors. Both s and r are neighbors of s'', and let $t = N(s, s'', r)$ (the other joint neighbor of s and r). By part i, $t \notin T(\to)$. If $t \in A$, then add $r \to t$. If $t \in R$, then delete $t \to t'$ (t' can be r!) and add $r \to t$ and $t \to s$. The new relation satisfies properties 1, 2, 4, and 7 but with one less element in A, which goes to a non-neighbor.

Go back to part i. Following a finite number of iterations we obtain a relation satisfying properties 1, 2, 3, and 4.

Finally, for every $s \in A$ for which $s \to t$ and there is no $r \to s$ for some $r \in R$, we can omit the arrow $s \to t$ to obtain a relation that satisfies property 5 as well. $\qquad\square$

Proposition 7. *The set A is implementable if and only if every connected component of R contains* (i) *a cycle or* (ii) *a profile r such that there are two profiles s, $t \in A$ and $rNsNt$.*

Proof.   Assume that A is implementable. By proposition 6, it is implementable by a canonical codex Λ, and by proposition 5 there is a binary relation $\to$ satisfying properties 1, 2, 3, 4, and 5. Consider a connected component Y of R. By properties 2 and 3, every $r \in Y$ has a neighbor $s(r)$ such that $r \to s(r)$. If for every $r \in Y$ the profile $s(r) \in R$, then Y must contain a cycle. Otherwise, there is an $r \in Y$ with $r \to s$ and $s \in A$. Then, by property 2, it must be that $s \in P(\to) - T(\to)$, and thus there must be some $t \in T(\to) \subseteq A$ such that $s \to t$ and by property 3 $rNsNt$.

In the other direction, let $Y_1, \ldots, Y_N$ be a sequence of all connected components of R. If $N = 0$, the set $A = S$ is truthfully implementable (proposition 3(1)). If $N > 0$, we inductively construct a relation $\to$ that at the end of stage $n - 1$ will satisfy properties 1, 3, 4, and 5 and $P(\to) = S - Y_1 \cup \cdots \cup Y_{n-1}$ as well as $P(\to) - T(\to) \subseteq A$ (and thus $Y_n \cup \cdots \cup Y_N \subseteq T(\to)$). At the end of stage $n = N$, we obtain a relation satisfying properties 1, 2, 3, 4, and 5, and by proposition 5 the set A is implementable.

We now describe the nth stage of the inductive construction of $\to$:

i. The modification of $\to$ for the case in which Y_n contains a cycle is straightforward (following the construction in proposition 2).

ii. If there exists $r \in Y_n$ that is a neighbor of $s \in P(\to) - T(\to)$, then we can extend the relation $\to$ by adding $r \to s$ and $\{x \to y \mid x \in Y_N$ and y is a neighbor of x on the path from x to $r\}$ (there is only one path from x to r since Y_n does not contain a cycle).

We can now concentrate on the case in which there is $r^* \in Y_n$ such that $r^* N s^* N t^*$ and $s^*, t^* \in A$, and there is no $r \in Y_n$ that has a neighbor $s \in P(\to) - T(\to)$.

iii. Next, we show that it can be assumed that there is no s such that $s \to s^*$.

If there is a profile s such that $s \to s^*$, then $s \notin R$ since if $s \in R$ it must be that $s^* \in P(\to) - T(\to)$, a situation already covered in part ii. Therefore, assume that $s \to s^*$ and $s \in A$. By property 5 of $\to$, there is $r \in R$ such that $r \to s$. The profile $x = N(r^*, s^*, s) \notin R$ since if $x \in R$ it must belong to Y_n and xNs, a case already covered in part ii. Also, $x \notin P(\to) - T(\to)$ since r^*Nx. Thus, $x \in T(\to)$, and we can delete $s \to s^*$ and add $s \to x$.

iv. We are left with the situation in which $r^*Ns^*Nt^*$, s^*, $t^* \in A$, $s^* \in T(\to)$, and there is no $s \to s^*$.

   If s^* has a neighbor x in $A \cap T(\to)$, then we can extend the relation $\to$ such that $r^* \to s^* \to x$ and for any other $r \in Y_N$ we can add $r \to s$ where $(r, s, \ldots, r^*)$ is the path from r to r^* in Y_N.
   Otherwise, t^*, which is in A, is not in $T(\to)$, and by property 5 there are some profiles in R that are directed to t^*.
   For every r such that $r \to t^*$, let $x(r) = N(r, t^*, s^*)$. We have already dealt with the case in which for at least one r we have $x(r) \in A \cap T(\to)$. We are left with two possibilities to consider:

a. If $x(r) \in P(\to) - T(\to)$, that is, there is $y \in A$ such that $x(r) \to y$, we can redirect $r \to x(r)$.
b. If $x(r) \in R$, it must be in $Y_1 \cup \cdots \cup Y_{n-1}$ since $x(r)Nr$ and $r \in Y_1 \cup \cdots \cup Y_{n-1}$. Then, for each such r redirect $r \to x(r)$ and $x(r) \to s^*$.

   There are no remaining profiles directed to t^*, and as before we can extend the relation such that $r^* \to s^* \to t^*$ and $\{r \to s \mid r \in Y_n$ and $(r, s, \ldots, r^*)$ is the path from r to r^* in $Y_N\}$. $\qquad \Box$

Corollary.

1. *If there exists $s^* \in R$ such that $A \supseteq N(s^*)$ and for any $x \in N(s^*)$ we have $N(x) \subseteq R$, then A is not implementable.*
2. *If all connected components of A are singletons and A is not truthfully implementable, then A is not implementable. The set $A = \{(0,1,0,0), (0,0,1,0), (0,0,0,1), (1,1,1,0), (1,1,0,1), (1,0,1,1)\}$ is an example of a set satisfying property 2 but not property 1 (the set $\{(0,0,0,0), (1,0,0,0), (1,1,0,0)\}$ is a connected component of R that does not have a cycle).*

   Using the above characterization, proposition 8 presents three families of implementable sets. In the first, each set A has the property that the truth of a particular variable in a profile guarantees that the profile is in A. The second consists of all sets A, each of which contains all but at most K profiles. The third consists of all sets A that have the property that if a profile s is in A then any other profile that agrees with s on the variables for which $s(v) = T$ is also in A (e.g., the set of all profiles in which $(v_1 \wedge v_2) \vee (v_3 \wedge v_4 \wedge v_5)$ is satisfied).

Proposition 8. *For $K \geq 3$, any set A that satisfies at least one of the following conditions is implementable:*

1. $A \supseteq T(v)$ *for some variable v (recall that $T(v)$ is the set of all profiles in which the variable v receives the value T);*
2. $|R| \leq K$;
3. *A is monotonic in the following sense: if $s \in A$ and s' is a profile such that, for every variable v, whenever $s(v) = T$ also $s'(v) = T$, then $s' \in A$.*

Proof.   Condition 1: Every profile $s \in R$ assigns the truth value F to the variable v and is a neighbor of a profile in $T(v)$, which has another neighbor in $T(v)$.

Condition 2: If $|R| \leq K$, then any $r \in R$ has a neighbor s in A, and if s does not have K neighbors in R, it must have a neighbor in A. If $R = N(s^*)$, then given $K \geq 3$ there is a ray $(s^*, r, n(r), n^2(r))$ and both $n(r)$ and $n^2(r)$ are in A.

Condition 3: The case $A = \{all\ truth\}$ is dealt with in proposition 3(1). Otherwise A is a connected set (all profiles are connected to *all truth*) that is not a singleton. The set R is connected (since if it is not empty all profiles are connected to *all false*). There must be a profile in R that is a neighbor of a profile in A, which in turn is a neighbor of another profile in A.   □

7. Discussion

Experimental Evidence

We obviously do not view the bounded rationality element in our model as an exact description of reality. Nevertheless, we believe that it captures some elements of real life. The following series of experiments provides some supporting evidence. Subjects from more than 30 countries who had all taken a game theory course and had registered on the site gametheory.tau.ac.il were asked to participate in a short Web-based experiment. The subjects were first asked the following three questions:

1. On most days, do you go to bed *before* midnight or *after* midnight?
2. Which of the following do you prefer: *cheese* cake or *chocolate* cake?
3. Were you born on an *odd* or *even* day of the month?

After answering the three questions, the subjects were presented with a new screen:

Assume now that as part of a marketing campaign you have been offered the chance to participate in a lottery. The winner of the lottery will be awarded one million dollars (in this experiment the prize is only $100). In order to be eligible to participate, you must answer three questions about yourself and your answers must not violate any of the following six restrictions [the restrictions were presented in random order]:

R1. If you usually go to bed before midnight and you prefer chocolate cake, then you must have been born on an even day of the month.

R2. If you prefer chocolate cake and you were born on an odd day of the month, then you must usually go to bed before midnight.

R3. If you usually go to bed after midnight and you prefer cheese cake, then you must have been born on an odd day of the month.

R4. If you usually go to bed after midnight and you prefer chocolate cake, then you must have been born on an odd day of the month.

R5. If you prefer cheese cake and you were born on an even day of the month, then you must usually go to bed after midnight.

R6. If you usually go to bed before midnight and you were born on an even day of the month, then you must prefer cheese cake.

Assume that you very much want to participate in the lottery and you know that the organizers have no way of verifying whether your answers are true. How would you answer the following three questions in this case?

1. Do you usually go to bed before or after midnight?
2. Which of the following do you prefer: cheese cake or chocolate cake?
3. Were you born on an odd or even day of the month?

Letting v_1 = "before midnight," v_2 = "cheese cake," and v_3 = "odd day of the month," the codex above, denoted by Λ_1, consists of six rules: $v_1 \wedge -v_2 \rightarrow -v_3$, $-v_2 \wedge v_3 \rightarrow v_1$, $-v_1 \wedge v_2 \rightarrow v_3$, $-v_1 \wedge -v_2 \rightarrow v_3$, $v_2 \wedge v_3 \rightarrow -v_1$, and $v_1 \wedge -v_3 \rightarrow v_2$. The induced guidance relation is $111 \rightarrow_{\Lambda_1} 011$, $100 \rightarrow_{\Lambda_1} 110$, $010 \rightarrow_{\Lambda_1} 011$, $101 \rightarrow_{\Lambda_1} 100$, $001 \rightarrow_{\Lambda_1} 101$, and $000 \rightarrow_{\Lambda_1} 001$. Thus, $T(\Lambda_1) = \{011, 110\}$ and $P(\Lambda_1) = T(\Lambda_1) \cup \{111, 100, 010\}$.

We partitioned the subjects into three groups, $T = T(\Lambda_1)$, $P = P(\Lambda_1) - T(\Lambda_1)$, and $R = R(\Lambda_1)$, according to their "declared profile" on the first screen. Each row in the following table refers to one of these groups.

The first column presents the proportion of subjects in each group whose answers in the second screen belong to T. The second column, denoted by "Honest," presents the proportion of subjects in each group who submitted the same profile in the second screen as in the first. (Notice that 9 percent of the subjects in T answered successfully by reporting the profile in T on the second screen, which is not the one they declared initially.) The third column, denoted by "Other," presents the proportion of subjects in each group whose answer was neither in T nor honest.

Λ_1	Success Rate (%)	Honest (%)	Other (%)	N
T	80	71	20	104
P	54	29	17	180
R	36	34	30	261

Following are our main observations.

1. The results support our basic assumption that the ability of a subject to come up with a persuasive profile strongly depends on his true profile. While 80 percent of the subjects in T submitted a persuasive profile, the success rate dropped to 54 percent among the subjects in P and to 36 percent among the subjects in R.

2. The median response time of successful subjects increased from 125s for subjects in T to 157s for subjects in P and even more dramatically to 317s for subjects in R. This supports our assumption that subjects in R find it more difficult to come up with a persuasive profile than subjects in P and T.

3. According to Λ_1, each of the three profiles in P is guided by the codex to a single profile in T (two are guided to 011 and one to 110). Indeed, of the 97 subjects in P who submitted a persuasive profile, 68 percent followed the guide. This result supports our main assumption that subjects use the codex as a guide in coming up with a persuasive profile using their true profile as a starting point.

4. The choices of the 251 subjects in $P \cup R$ who failed to submit a persuasive profile are far from being random. Of these subjects, 56 percent were honest while 35 percent chose a profile that is confirmed by a rule in the codex, in the sense that the profile satisfies both its antecedent and its

consequent (100, 101, or 001). Only 9 percent chose a profile that was not confirmed by any of the rules (111, 010, or 000).

5. One could suggest an alternative model of bounded rationality according to which a subject considers only his true profile and the (three) neighboring ones. However, the results do not support this hypothesis. First, note that for subjects with the true profiles 111 and 010, the two persuasive profiles are neighboring ones. However, they are guided by the codex only to 011 (and not to 110). Indeed, 75 percent of the 72 subjects who submitted a persuasive profile followed the guide and chose 011. Second, the success rate of the 001 subjects (37 percent) who had a neighboring profile in T was no different from those for the other two R profiles (101 and 000), which do not have a neighboring profile in T (37 percent and 33 percent, respectively).

An alternative explanation for the popularity of 011 among the 111 and 010 subjects is that 011 is confirmed by two rules. Therefore, we conducted a second experiment with a modified codex, denoted by Λ_2, whose guidance relation is $111 \rightarrow_{\Lambda_2} 011$, $100 \rightarrow_{\Lambda_2} 110$, $010 \rightarrow_{\Lambda_2} 110$, $001 \rightarrow_{\Lambda_2} 011$, $101 \rightarrow_{\Lambda_2} 100$, and $000 \rightarrow_{\Lambda_2} 001$. For this codex, $T(\Lambda_2) = T(\Lambda_1)$, but $P(\Lambda_2) - T(\Lambda_2)$ consists of four profiles: 111 and 001 (guided by the codex to 011) and 100 and 010 (guided to 110). The following table summarizes the main results:

Λ_2	Success Rate (%)	Honest (%)	Other (%)	N
T	88	75	12	52
P	63	27	10	123
R	45	15	40	65

Once again, we observe a strong dependence of the success rate on the subject's true profile. Almost all T profiles, 63 percent of the P profiles, and only 45 percent of the R profiles came up with a persuasive profile. Particularly interesting is the group of 123 subjects whose profile is in P. Each of the four profiles in P is guided by the codex to a unique profile in T. Of the 78 successful subjects in P, 51 subjects (65 percent) seem to have been guided by the codex. We believe that this result strongly supports our main assumption that individuals first determine whether their true profile satisfies the codex, and if it does not then they consider a profile to which they are guided by the codex.

Finally, we also tried another codex, denoted by Λ_3, which truthfully implements $\{110, 011\}$. The induced guidance relation is $111 \rightarrow_{\Lambda 3} 101$, $100 \rightarrow_{\Lambda 3} 101$, $010 \rightarrow_{\Lambda 3} 000$, $101 \rightarrow_{\Lambda 3} 100$, $001 \rightarrow_{\Lambda 3} 101$, and $000 \rightarrow_{\Lambda 3} 001$. The following table summarizes the results:

Λ_3	T (%)	Honest (%)	Other (%)	N
T	81	77	19	26
R	34	44	22	100

Once again, there is a dramatic difference between the success rates of the T's (81 percent) and the R's (34 percent). The Rs' success rate and their median response time ($332s$) are similar to those of the R's in the previous experiments, and only one R subject chose a profile not confirmed by any of the rules in the codex.

Related Literature

The idea that cheating is difficult is, of course, not a new one. Within the economic literature, it appears in Kamien and Zemel (1990), among others. They reinterpreted Cook's theorem (see Cook 1971), which proves that deciding whether a given Boolean formula in conjunctive normal form has an assignment that makes the formula true is an NP-complete problem.

Kartik (2009) analyzed a model of persuasion in which a speaker incurs a cost if he chooses to misrepresent his private information. Inflated language naturally arises in this environment.

The idea that the framing of a mechanism may also provide some guidance to the participants appeared in Glazer and Rubinstein (1996). In that paper, we introduced the concept of implementation via guided iterative elimination of dominated strategies in a normal form game and showed that it is equivalent to "implementation using a subgame perfect equilibrium of an extensive game with perfect information."

The idea that the mechanism itself can affect agents' preferences and thus the implementability of social outcomes appears in Glazer and Rubinstein (1998). In that paper, a number of experts receive noisy signals regarding a public decision. Two "cultures" were compared: In the first, the experts are driven only by the public motive to increase the probability that the desirable action will be taken. In the second, each expert is also driven by a private motive to have his recommendation adopted. We show that only the second culture gives rise to a mechanism whose unique equilibrium outcome achieves the public target.

A model of implementation with boundedly rational agents was presented by Eliaz (2002), who investigated the implementation problem when some of the agents are "faulty" in the sense that they fail to act optimally. Eliaz introduces a solution concept called "fault-tolerant implementation," which requires robustness to deviations from equilibrium, and shows that under symmetric information any choice rule that satisfies certain properties can be implemented if the number of faulty players is sufficiently small. In Cabrales and Serrano (2011), there must exist a mechanism that induces players' actions to converge to the desired outcome when they follow best-response dynamics in order for a social choice function to be implementable. De Clippel (2011) expands standard implementation theory by assuming that agents' decisions are determined by choice functions that are not necessarily rationalizable.

Conclusion

The model presented here facilitates the analysis of some basic consid- erations used by a principal in attempting to elicit information from an agent who may have an incentive to cheat. The principal would like the mechanism to be complex enough that an agent, whose interests clash with his own, will not be guided by the mechanism itself to successfully distort the information he is conveying. At the same time, the principal would like the mechanism to be simple enough that an agent whose interests coincide with his own will be able to persuade him. Following are some of our main insights.

1. In some cases, it is optimal for the listener to use a codex that will help the speaker "alter the truth," that is, present a false but persuasive profile. This result is consistent with the casual observation that some exaggeration is sometimes viewed as necessary in real-life situations (see Kartik, Ottaviani, and Squintani 2007).
2. If the circumstances under which the listener should (from his point of view) accept the speaker's request are rare, then truthful implementation is easy. This will be accomplished by means of a codex that will trap all "undeserving" speakers (i.e., speakers whose profile should not be accepted) in a "circle of lies." In other words, an undeserving speaker

is (mis) guided by the codex to pretend to be another undeserving speaker whose profile is rejected by the codex and who, in turn, is guided by the codex to pretend to be a third undeserving speaker whose profile is rejected and so on. This procedure continues until one of the undeserving speakers is guided by the codex to present a profile that appears previously in the chain.

3. If the circumstances under which the listener should reject the speaker's request are rare, then the optimal mechanism requires the speaker, in some circumstances, to cheat successfully. This occurs because the codex sometimes guides a speaker with an undeserving profile to pretend to be a speaker with a deserving one, who himself is rejected by the codex but is guided to another profile that is accepted.

Most importantly, the paper suggests a new direction for the study of mechanism design with boundedly rational agents.

References

Cabrales, Antonio, and Roberto Serrano. 2011. "Implementation in Adaptive Better-Response Dynamics: Towards a General Theory of Bounded Rationality in Mechanism." *Games and Econ. Behavior* 73:360–74.

Cook, Stephen A. 1971. "The Complexity of Theorem Proving Procedures." In *Proceedings Third Annual ACM Symposium on Theory of Computing*, 151–58. New York: ACM.

de Clippel, Geoffroy. 2011. "Behavioral Implementation." Discussion paper, Brown Univ.

Eliaz, Kfir. 2002. "Fault Tolerant Implementation." *Rev. Econ. Studies* 69:589–610.

Glazer, Jacob, and Ariel Rubinstein. 1996. "An Extensive Game as a Guide for Solving a Normal Game." *J. Econ. Theory* 70:32–42.

———. 1998. "Motives and Implementation: On the Design of Mechanisms to Elicit Opinions." *J. Econ. Theory* 79:157–73.

———. 2004. "On Optimal Rules of Persuasion." *Econometrica* 72:1715–36.

———. 2006. "A Study in the Pragmatics of Persuasion: A Game Theoretical Approach." *Theoretical Econ.* 1:395–410.

Green, Jerry R., and Jean Jacques Laffont. 1986. "Partially Verifiable Information and Mechanism Design." *Rev. Econ. Studies* 53:447–56.

Kamien, Morton I., and Eitan Zemel. 1990. "Tangled Webs: A Note on the Complexity of Compound Lying." Manuscript, Northwestern Univ.

Kartik, Navin. 2009. "Strategic Communication with Lying Costs." *Rev. Econ. Studies* 76:1359–95.

Kartik, Navin, Marco Ottaviani, and Francesco Squintani. 2007. "Credulity, Lies, and Costly Talk." *J. Econ. Theory* 134:93–116.

Chapter 7

Complex Questionnaires

Jacob Glazer

Faculty of Management,
Tel Aviv University, Tel Aviv 69978,
Israel and Dept. of Economics,
University of Warwick, Coventry, CV4 7AL, U.K.;
glazer@post.tau.ac.il

Ariel Rubinstein*

School of Economics,
Tel Aviv University, Tel Aviv 69978,
Israel and Dept. of Economics,
New York University, New York, NY 10012, U.S.A.;
rariel@post.tau.ac.il

We study a principal-agent model in which the agent is boundedly rational in his ability to understand the principal's decision rule. The principal wishes to elicit an agent's true profile so as to determine whether or not to grant him a certain request. The principal designs a questionnaire and commits himself to accepting certain responses. In designing such a questionnaire, the principal takes into account the bounded rationality of the agent and wishes to reduce the success probability of a dishonest agent who is trying to game the system. It is shown that the principal can construct a sufficiently complex questionnaire that will allow him to respond optimally to agents who tell the truth and at the same time to almost eliminate the probability that a dishonest agent will succeed in cheating.

Keywords: Bounded rationality, persuasion games, questionnaires.

*The first author thanks the Henry Crown Institute of Business Research in Israel for its financial support. The second author acknowledges financial support in the form of ERC Grant 269143. Our thanks to Noga Alon, Gil Kalai, Xiaosheng Mu, Neil Thakral, and Tal Rabin for their advice on combinatorial issues.

1. Introduction

In many principal-agent situations, a principal makes a decision based on information provided to him by an agent. Since the agent and the principal do not necessarily share the same objectives, the principal cannot simply ask the agent to provide him with the relevant information (hereafter referred to as the agent's profile). He instead must utilize an additional tool to induce the agent to provide accurate information. The economic literature has focused on two such tools: verification (requiring the agent to present hard evidence) and incentives (rewarding or penalizing the agent on the basis of the information he provides). However, these tools are often prohibitively expensive or insufficient to achieve the task.

The purpose of this paper is to analyze a different type of tool that can be used by a principal to reduce the probability of an agent cheating successfully. Instead of asking the agent direct questions to elicit the relevant information, the principal can design a sufficiently complex questionnaire such that a boundedly rational agent who is considering lying will find it difficult to come up with consistent answers that will induce the principal to take an action desired by the agent.

The analysis is carried out in the context of a simple persuasion model. A principal interacts on a routine basis with many different agents who present him with requests. In each case, the principal must decide whether or not to accept the request. He would like to accept the request if and only if the agent's profile meets certain conditions, whereas the agent would like his request to be accepted regardless of his true profile. The agent's profile is known only to himself and cannot be verified by the principal. To obtain the information he needs, the principal designs a questionnaire for the agent that contains a set of yes/no questions regarding his profile. The principal accepts the agent's request if the agent's response to the questionnaire (i.e., the list of answers he provides) is included within a set of acceptable responses.

At the core of our model are assumptions regarding the procedure used by a boundedly rational agent, who instead of answering the questionnaire honestly attempts to come up with a response that will be accepted. We assume that the agent does not know (or does not fully understand) the principal's policy (i.e., which responses to the questionnaire will be accepted). However, the agent can detect (or is able to understand or is informed of) certain interdependencies between the answers to the various questions in the set of acceptable responses. We refer to such an interdependency as a *regularity*. An agent is characterized by the level of regularities he can detect. The most boundedly rational agent (an agent of level 0) is only able to determine whether an answer to a particular question must be positive or negative. An agent of level d will be able to determine whether, within the set of acceptable responses, an answer to a set of d questions uniquely determines the answer to an additional question.

Note that we assume the agents can detect regularities in the set of acceptable responses but cannot imitate any particular acceptable response. What we have in mind is that the agent perceives the set of acceptable responses in an analogous way to how a person views a picture of an orchard during fruit picking season. An unsophisticated observer will only be able to see that the picture is green. A more observant individual will notice that the pixels form the shapes of trees. A really astute individual will notice that next to each tree with fruit on it, there is a person with a ladder. Even the most observant individuals, however, will not be able to draw or recall even a tiny part of the picture later on.

The principal's goal in designing the questionnaire is twofold: his first priority is to make the right decision (from his point of view) when an agent answers the questionnaire honestly. His second priority is to minimize the acceptance probability of a dishonest agent who has abandoned his true profile and, based on the regularities he detects in the set of acceptable responses, tries to guess an acceptable answer. We demonstrate that a complex questionnaire can serve as a tool for the principal to achieve these two goals. The principal's optimal questionnaire depends on the agent's level of bounded rationality. The more boundedly rational the agent is, the lower will be the probability that he will succeed in dishonestly responding to the optimal questionnaire.

Following the construction and discussion of the model, we prove two main results: (i) if the principal uses an optimal questionnaire, a dishonest agent's ability to come up with an acceptable answer depends only on the size of the set of profiles that the principal wishes to accept, and (ii) when the set of acceptable profiles is large, the principal can design a questionnaire that will reduce to almost zero the probability of a dishonest agent cheating effectively.

2. The Model

The Principal and the Agent

The agent possesses private information, referred to as his true *profile*, in the form of an element ω in a finite set Ω. The principal needs to choose between two actions: a (accept) and r (reject). The agent would like the principal to choose the action a, regardless of his true profile. The principal's desired action depends on the agent's true profile: he wishes to choose a if the agent's profile belongs to a set A, a proper subset of Ω, and to choose r if the profile is in $R = \Omega - A$. Denote the size of A by n. A persuasion problem is a pair (Ω, A).

A Questionnaire

A questionnaire is a (multi)set of questions. Each question is of the form, "Does your profile belong to the set q?" where $q \subset \Omega$. We will denote the question according to the set that the question asks about.

The agent responds to each question with a "yes" (1) or a "no" (0). The principal does not know the agent's profile and cannot verify any of the answers given by him.

Following are two examples of questionnaires:

(i) The *one-click* questionnaire, which consists of $|\Omega|$ questions of the form $\{\omega\}$. That is, each question asks whether the agent has a particular profile.

(ii) Let $\Omega = \{0,1\}^K$. A profile contains information about K relevant binary characteristics. The *simple* questionnaire consists of K questions, each of which asks about a distinct characteristic, that is, $q_k = \{w | w_k = 1\}$.

A *response* to a questionnaire Q is a function that assigns a value of 1 or 0 to each question in Q. It will sometimes be convenient to order the questions in Q (i.e., $(q_1, \ldots, q_L)$) and to identify a response using an L-vector of 0's and 1's. Let $\Theta(Q)$ be the set of all possible responses to Q. Let $\theta(Q, \omega)$ be the response to Q given by an honest agent whose profile is ω, that is, the vector of length L whose ith component is 1 if $\omega \in q_i$ and 0 otherwise.

For every A and Q, define the following three sets:

(i) $\Theta(Q, A) = \{\theta(Q, \omega) | \omega \in A\}$ (the set of honest responses given by agents whose profiles are in A).

(ii) $\Theta(Q, R) = \{\theta(Q, \omega) | \omega \in \Omega - A\}$ (the set of honest responses given by agents whose profiles are in R).

(iii) Inconsistent $(Q) = \Theta(Q) - \{\Theta(Q, \omega) | \omega \in \Omega\}$ (the set of responses that are not given by any honest agent).

We say that a questionnaire Q *identifies* A if, when all agents are honest, the responses of the agents whose profiles are in A differ from the responses of the agents whose profiles are in R (that is, $\Theta(Q, A) \cap \Theta(Q, R) = \emptyset$). The one-click questionnaire (as well as the simple questionnaire) identifies any set A, since any two profiles induce two different responses.

An agent does not know the set of acceptable responses. We assume that he is either (i) honest in the sense that he automatically tells the truth or (ii) a manipulator who, regardless of his true profile, tries to respond to the questionnaire successfully after learning some properties of the set of acceptable responses.

We assume that the principal's first priority is to accept honest agents whose profile is in A and to reject all others. In other words, he seeks a questionnaire that identifies A and adheres to a policy of accepting a response if and only if it is in $\Theta(Q, A)$. The principal's second priority is to design a questionnaire that makes it less likely for a manipulator to come up with an acceptable answer.

The Bounded Rationality Element

At the core of our model is the element of bounded rationality. Were a manipulative agent fully aware of the set of acceptable responses, $\Theta(Q, A)$, he would always choose an acceptable response and the principal would be helpless. However, we assume that an agent is limited in his ability to figure out the set $\Theta(Q, A)$ and does not have any prior beliefs on it. In the spirit of the set theoretic model of knowledge, we assume that an agent detects certain types of regularities in the set. By *regularity*, we are referring to a sentence (in the language of propositional logic with the variables being the names of the questions in Q) that is true in $\Theta(Q, A)$. The agent detects regularities but is not able to cite any particular acceptable response. This phenomenon is common in real life. For example, the fact that we observe that all papers accepted to *Econometrica* contain formal models does not mean that we are able to cite any of them.

The set of regularities detected by an agent is characterized by a rank, which is an integer $d \geq 0$. An agent of rank d can recognize propositions of the form $\varphi_1 \rightarrow \varphi_2$, where the antecedent φ_1 is a conjunction of at most d clauses, each of which is an affirmation or a negation of a question, and the consequent φ_2 is a question (which does not appear in the antecedent) or its negation. We will refer to such a proposition as a d-implication. Given a questionnaire Q, an agent of rank d can figure out all the d-implications that are true for all responses in $\Theta(Q, A)$. Thus, an agent of rank 0 observes only regularities such as "In all accepted responses, the answer to the question q is N" (denoted $-q$). An agent of rank 1 is also able to identify regularities of the type "In all accepted responses, if the answer to q_1 is N, then the answer to q_3 is Y" (denoted $-q_1 \to q_3$). The propositions $-q_1 \wedge -q_2 \to q_3$ constitute an example of a regularity of rank 2.

Let $\Theta_d(Q, A)$ be the set of responses that satisfy all the d-implications that are true for all responses in $\Theta(Q, A)$. By definition, $\Theta_d(Q, A) \supseteq \Theta_{d+1}(Q, A) \supseteq \Theta(Q, A)$ for all d.

We assume that if instead of responding honestly to the questionnaire, an agent of rank d is interested in gaming the system (i.e., coming up with a response in $\Theta(Q, A)$, regardless of his true profile), he will choose randomly from among the responses in $\Theta_d(Q, A)$. His probability of success is, therefore, $\alpha_d(Q, A) = |\Theta(Q, A)| / |\Theta_d(A, Q)|$. Obviously, $\alpha_d(Q, A)$ is weakly increasing in d.

The Principal's Problem

As mentioned, the principal has two objectives in designing a questionnaire: His lexicographically first priority is to accept honest agents whose profile is in A and to reject all others. Hence, the questionnaire needs to identify A and the principal's policy should be to accept only responses given by honest agents whose profile is in A. His second priority is to minimize the probability that a manipulator will be able to successfully deceive him (i.e., the principal wishes to minimize $\alpha_d(Q, A)$). In other words, the principal's problem is

$$\min\{\alpha_d(Q, A) | Q \text{ identifies } A\}.$$

The value of this optimization is denoted by $\beta_d(A)$.

Note that we are not following the standard mechanism design approach according to which the principal faces a distribution of agents' types and seeks a policy that maximizes the principal's expected payoff.

Example 1. Recall that the one-click questionnaire, *oneclick*, contains $|\Omega|$ questions (of the form $\{\omega\}$), one for each profile. The set $\Theta(oneclick, A)$ consists of all responses that assign the value 1 to precisely one question $\{\omega\}$, where $\omega \in A$.

An agent of rank 0 will learn to answer 0 to all the questions related to profiles in R. If A contains at least two profiles, the agent will learn nothing about how to respond to questions regarding profiles in A and thus $\alpha_0(Q, A) = n/2^n$ (where $n = |A|$).

An agent of rank 1 will, in addition, observe the regularities $\{\omega\} \rightarrow -\{\omega'\}$, where $\omega \in A$ and $\omega \neq \omega'$. For $n > 2$, the agent will not detect any additional regularities and, therefore, $\Theta_1(oneclick, A)$ consists of the set $\Theta(oneclick, A)$ and the "constant 0" response. Hence, $\alpha_1(oneclick, A) = n/(n+1)$. For $n = 2$, we have in addition $-\{\omega\} \rightarrow \{\omega'\}$ and, therefore, $\alpha_1(oneclick, A) = 1$.

Example 2. We have in mind that a question is not necessarily phrased directly, but rather in an equivalent indirect way as demonstrated in the following example:

A principal would like to identify scholars who are interested in at least two of the following three fields: law, economics, and history. Thus, a profile can be presented as a triple of 0's and 1's, indicating whether or not an agent is interested in each field ($\Omega = \{0, 1\}^3$), and A is the set of the four profiles in which at least two characteristics receive the value 1.

The principal can simply ask the agent three questions:

1. Are you interested in law?
2. Are you interested in economics?
3. Are you interested in history?

This is formalized as the simple questionnaire $Q = \{q_1, q_2, q_3\}$, where q_i is the question about dimension i. The set of acceptable responses is $\Theta(Q, A) = \{(1, 1, 1), (1, 1, 0), (0, 1, 1), (1, 0, 1)\}$. The set $\Theta(Q, R)$ consists of all other possible responses.

An agent with $d = 0$ cannot detect any regularity in the set of acceptable responses since interest in any particular field or lack thereof is not a necessary requirement for a response to be accepted. That is, neither q nor $-q$ is true in $\Theta(Q, A)$. Thus, $\alpha_0(Q, A) = 1/2$.

An agent with $d = 1$ realizes that if he says he is not interested in one field, then he should say that he is interested in the other two. That is, the 1-implications that are true in $\Theta(Q, A)$ are the six propositions $-q_j \rightarrow q_k$, where $j \neq k$. The set of responses that satisfy these six propositions ($\Theta_1(Q, A)$) is exactly $\Theta(Q, A)$. Thus, an agent with $d = 1$ will fully understand the set of acceptable responses, that is, $\alpha_1(Q, A) = 1$.

Suppose that instead of asking these three questions, the principal uses the following questionnaire:

1. Are you familiar with the book *Sex and Reason?*
2. Are you familiar with the book *The Book Club Murder?*
3. Are you familiar with the book *Which Road to the Past?*

The first book was written by Richard Posner, a leading figure in law and economics. The second book was written by Lawrence Friedman, a well known scholar who bridges between law and history. The author of the third book is the prominent economic historian Robert Fogel. Thus, each book spans two of the three fields. For example, a scholar will be familiar with *Sex and Reason* if and only if he is interested in both law and economics.

Notice that the acceptable responses to this questionnaire are either three yes's or a single yes. An agent with $d = 1$ cannot detect whether an answer of yes or no to one question implies anything about the other two.

Formally, let Q' be the questionnaire $\{q_{12}, q_{13}, q_{23}\}$, where q_{ij} asks whether the ith and jth characteristics have the value 1, that is, $q_{ij} = \{\omega | \omega_i = \omega_j = 1\}$. The questionnaire Q' identifies A as $\Theta(Q', A) = \{(1,1,1), (1,0,0), (0,1,0), (0,0,1)\}$ and $\Theta(Q', R) = \{(0,0,0)\}$. No 1-implication is true in $\Theta(Q', A)$, and thus $\Theta_1(Q', A)$ contains all eight possible responses and $\alpha_1(Q', A) = 1/2$. As we will see later, the principal can do even better and reduce this probability to $1/3$.

Notice that an agent with $d = 2$ realizes that any one of the four combinations of answers to q_{12} and q_{13} in the set of acceptable responses uniquely determines the answer to q_{23}, and thus $\Theta_2(Q', A) = \Theta(Q', A)$ and $\alpha_2(Q', A) = 1$.

3. Comments on the Bounded Rationality Element

As always, when one departs from the model of the ultra-rational economic agent, special assumptions are necessary. We believe that our model captures some interesting aspects of the situation we have in mind, although there are other assumptions that could be made and that would also yield interesting results. In what follows, we discuss the assumptions made regarding the agent's bounded rationality.

a. *What does the agent see?* The agent focuses on the space of responses without being able to relate to the space of profiles. If he was capable of "inferring backward" from the space of responses to the space of profiles, he could probably determine the set A and come up with an acceptable response to the questionnaire, as if he indeed possessed one of the profiles in A. Furthermore, since the agent does not relate to the space of profiles, he is not capable of identifying inconsistent responses.

The question of whether a questionnaire can conceal the interest of the principal in differentiating between profiles in A and profiles in R

depends on the language available to the principal when framing the questions. In Example 2, the question q_{12} can be framed in two different ways: (i) "Are you interested in both economics and law?" and (ii) "Are you familiar with the book *Sex and Reason*?" The availability of the second option makes the second questionnaire more attractive as a tool to elicit the agent's information without hinting to the agent regarding the principal's real interest.

b. *What does the agent notice in the set of acceptable responses?* Our key assumption is that the agent notices only certain regularities in the set of acceptable responses. A regularity of rank d is a dependency (within the set of acceptable responses) of the answer to one question on the answers to some d other questions. An agent with $d \geq 1$ is able to detect the regularity $q_1 \rightarrow q_2$ whenever such a regularity is true in the set $\Theta(Q, A)$. Notice that such a regularity is true even if there is no acceptable response to Q with a positive answer to q_1. An alternative assumption would be that the agent discerns such a regularity if in addition to it being logically true, there exists at least one acceptable response with affirmative answers to q_1 and q_2. For example, the regularity "All acceptable economists are theoreticians" is true if the acceptable set does not include any economists. However, under the alternative assumption, the agent would detect this regularity only if there exists one acceptable response containing an affirmative answer to the question "Are you an economist?"

Another plausible assumption would be that the agent can detect statistical correlations such as "Among the acceptable responses, 80% of those who answer yes to q_1 answered yes to q_2 as well."

c. *What does the agent not notice?* We assume that the regularities are observed in the set of acceptable responses but not in the set of rejected responses. This appears to a be reasonable assumption in cases where the agent notices information about agents whose request has been accepted (such as job candidates who have been hired), but not about those whose request has been rejected (those who did not get hired).

Furthermore, the agent does not understand that if his response satisfies a certain proposition his request will be accepted. This is a reasonable assumption in situations where it is easier for people to observe that, for example, "all admitted students are males" rather than "all males who applied were admitted."

d. *An agent is not able to exactly imitate an acceptable profile.* Possession of information about the set of acceptable responses does not necessarily imply familiarity with any particular acceptable response that can be copied. For example, assume you want to sneak into a party that you were not invited to. If you are an agent with $d = 0$ who thinks that what you are wearing is relevant to getting into the party, you will notice that all guests are wearing military uniforms and, therefore, you will not arrive at the party in a business suit. If you are an agent with $d = 1$, you will also notice that everyone wearing a white uniform is also wearing a navy emblem and thus you will either not arrive in a white uniform or you will wear a navy emblem if you do. However, this does not mean that you know exactly what combination of uniforms, emblems and insignia will keep you from getting caught and it will be impossible for you to duplicate every detail of what any one of the admitted guests is wearing.

This is captured by our assumption that an agent is unable to exactly imitate an acceptable response even though he knows some regularities about the set of acceptable responses. This assumption is also appropriate in situations where the agent is able to obtain partial information from people who have access to the file of acceptable responses without he himself having access.

e. *Framing our model as a conventional model of knowledge.* The agent's problem can be framed as a standard model of knowledge if we define the set of *feasible states* as the set of all nonempty sets of responses. A state is interpreted as the set of acceptable responses used by the principal. Applying our assumption to this framework would mean that the agent learns that certain responses do not belong to the set of accepted responses. Thus, for example, he cannot determine that there are three acceptable responses or that in 60% of the acceptable responses to a certain question the answer is yes. Given this kind of knowledge, an agent of rank d is able to determine that the acceptable set of responses can be any nonempty subset of $\Theta_d(Q, A)$. If his prior does not discriminate between the responses, he will conclude that any response in $\Theta_d(Q, A)$ is equally likely to be accepted and that any response outside this set will be rejected.

4. Some Observations

The following claim embodies some simple observations about $\alpha_d(Q, A)$.

Claim 1. (i) *If a combination of answers to m questions in Q never appears in $\Theta(Q, A)$, then such a combination will not appear in any element of $\Theta_d(Q, A)$ for $d \geq m - 1$. (For example, if the response of "yes to all" to the questions q_1, q_2, and q_3 does not appear in $\Theta(Q, A)$, then an agent with $d \geq 2$ will detect the regularity $q_1 \wedge q_2 \rightarrow q_3$.)*

(ii) *If Q consists of m questions, then $\alpha_d(Q, A) \equiv 1$ for all $d \geq m - 1$ (follows from (i)).*

(iii) *If the answer to q' is the same for all $\omega \in A$ (that is, if $q' \supseteq A$ or $-q' \supseteq A$), then $\alpha_d(Q, A) = \alpha_d(Q \cup \{q'\}, A)$ for all d.*

(iv) *Suppose that Q is a questionnaire that identifies A. Let Q' be a questionnaire obtained from Q by replacing one of the questions $q \in Q$ with $-q$. Then Q' identifies A and $\alpha_d(Q, A) = \alpha_d(Q', A)$ for all d.*

Claim 2 states that the principal can limit himself to questionnaires that are covers of A (where a questionnaire Q is a cover of A if for all $q \in Q$, $q \subseteq A$ and $\bigcup_{q \in Q} q = A$) and that $\beta_d(A)$ depends only on the size of A (and not on $|\Omega|$).

Claim 2. (i) *If Q identifies A, then there exists a questionnaire Q', which is a cover of A, that identifies A and $\alpha_d(Q, A) = \alpha_d(Q', A)$ for all d.*

(ii) *$\beta_d(A)$ is a function of $n = |A|$ and is independent of $|\Omega|$.*

Proof. (i) Consider $b \in R$. Since Q identifies A, then b's honest response to Q is different from that of any profile in A. By Claim 1(iv), we can assume that $b \notin q$ for all $q \in Q$, that is, b's honest response to the questionnaire is a constant 0. Since the questionnaire identifies A, every element in A belongs to at least one $q \in Q$.

Now let Q' be the questionnaire $\{q \cap A|$ there exists $q \in Q\}$. Q' identifies A: a response to Q' by a profile outside of A is a constant 0; a profile in A belongs to at least one $q' \in Q'$ and thus Q' is a cover of A. The honest response of each profile in A to any $q \in Q$ is the same as its honest response to $q \cap A \in Q'$ and, therefore, $\alpha_d(Q, A) = \alpha_d(Q', A)$.

(ii) By (i), we can assume that the optimal questionnaire is a cover of A and thus the size of R is immaterial for any $\alpha_d(Q, A)$. $\square$

Claim 3 states that the ability of the principal to prevent dishonest agents from successfully cheating depends on the relation between n and d. Thus, if $d \geq n - 1$, then a dishonest agent will be able to fully game the system.

Claim 3. $\alpha_{n-1}(Q, A) = 1$ *for all* Q.

Proof. Let $\Theta(Q, A) = \{z^1, \ldots, z^m\}$, where $m \leq n$. The claim is trivial for the case of $m = 1$. Otherwise, we could (inductively) construct a set of $m - 1$ questions in Q, such that for any profile in A, an honest answer to these questions would determine the honest answers to all the others.

In the first stage, let q be a question for which $z^1(q) \neq z^2(q)$. Define $Q(1) = \{q\}$. In $\{z^1, z^2\}$, the answer to q determines the responses to all other questions in Q.

By the end of the $(t-1)$th stage, we have a set $Q(t-1)$ of at most $t-1$ questions such that in $\{z^1, \ldots, z^t\}$, a response to these questions uniquely determines the responses to all the others.

In the tth stage, consider z^{t+1}. If for every $z^s (s \leq t)$, there is a question $q \in Q(t-1)$ such that $z^{t+1}(q) \neq z^s(q)$ (that is, if a "signature" of z^{t+1} appears in the answers to $Q(t-1)$), then $Q(t) = Q(t-1)$. If for some $s \leq t$, $z^{t+1}(q) = z^s(q)$ for all q in $Q(t-1)$, then there must be a question $q \notin Q(t-1)$ for which $z^{t+1}(q) \neq z^s(q)$. Let $Q(t) = Q(t-1) \cup \{q\}$. The answers to the (at most t) questions in $Q(t)$ uniquely determine the responses to all other questions in $\{z^1, \ldots, z^{t+1}\}$.

Finally, we reach the set $Q(m-1)$ of at most $(m-1)$ questions. Given that $d \geq n - 1 \geq m - 1$, the agent detects all the dependencies of the answer to any question outside $Q(m-1)$ on the response to the questions in $Q(m-1)$. Furthermore, he is able to detect any combination of responses to $Q(m-1)$ that never appear in $\Theta(Q, A)$. Thus, $\alpha_{n-1}(Q, A) = 1$. □

Comments: (a) We use the above claims to find an optimal questionnaire and to calculate $\beta_d(A)$ for $d = 1$ and some small values of n:

(i) From Claim 3, if $n \leq 2$, then $\beta_1(A) = 1$.

(ii) If $n = 3$, the one-click questionnaire is optimal and $\beta_1(A) = 3/4$. To see this, let Q be an optimal questionnaire. By Claim 1(iii), we can assume that neither of the questions receives a constant truth value. Since $d > 0$, we can assume that no two questions receive identical or opposing truth values for profiles in A and thus Q is a set of singletons. By Claim 1(ii), Q contains at least three questions. Thus, $\alpha_1(Q, A) = \alpha_1$ (*one click*, A).

(iii) If $A = \{a, b, c, d\}$, then $Q^* = (\{a, b\}, \{a, c\}, \{a, d\}, \{a\}, \{b\}, \{c\}, \{d\})$ is an optimal questionnaire and $\beta_1(A) = 1/3$. To see this, note that the four accepted responses to Q are

$$(1,1,1,1,0,0,0),$$
$$(1,0,0,0,1,0,0),$$
$$(0,1,0,0,0,1,0),$$
$$(0,0,1,0,0,0,1).$$

The question $\{\omega\}$ "identifies" ω. That is, for any question q, we have $\{\omega\} \to q$ if $\omega \in q$ and $\{\omega\} \to -q$ if $\omega \notin q$. Thus, $\Theta(Q^*, A)$ consists of the four honest responses given by profiles in A, and the eight responses that answer the last four questions negatively and the first three questions with an arbitrary combination of truth values. Thus, $\alpha_1(Q^*, A) = 1/3$.

To show that $\alpha_1(Q, A) \geq 1/3$ for all Q that identify A, we can assume that Q is a cover of A. By Claim 1, we can assume that $Q = Q_1 \cup Q_2$, where Q_k consists of sets of size k, and that $|Q_1| \leq 4$ and $|Q_2| \leq 3$. Each affirmative response to a question $\{\omega\} \in Q_1$ determines (in $\Theta(Q, A)$) the answers to all other questions. Thus, the set $\Theta_1(Q, A)$ contains at most the four responses of members of A and at most $2^{|Q_2|}$ responses θ for which $\theta(q) = 0$ for all $q \in Q_1$. Thus, $|\Theta_1(Q, A)| \leq |Q_1| + 2^{|Q_2|} \leq 12$ and $\alpha_1(Q, A) \geq 4/12$.

(b) Increasing the number of questions may *increase* the probability that a manipulator will succeed. Consider the case of $A = \{a, b, c, d\}$. Let $Q_1 = \{\{a, b\}, \{c\}, \{d\}\}$ and $Q_2 = \{\{a, b\}, \{c\}, \{d\}, \{a\}\}$. Then $\Theta(Q_1, A) = \{(1,0,0), (0,1,0), (0,0,1)\}$ and $\Theta_1(Q_i, A) = \Theta(Q_1, A) \cup \{(0,0,0)\}$, and thus $\alpha_1(Q_1, A) = 3/4$. However, $\Theta(Q_2, A) = \{(1,0,0,1), (1,0,0,0), (0,1,0,0), (0,0,1,0)\}$, $\Theta_1(Q_2, A) = \Theta(Q_2, A) \cup \{(0,0,0,0)\}$, and thus $\alpha_1(Q_2, A) = 4/5$.

5. Preventing (Almost All) Successful Cheating

Our last claim states that whatever the value of d, $\beta_d(A)$ decreases very rapidly with the size of A. The proof uses a concept from combinatorics: a collection C of subsets of A is said to be k-*independent* if for every k distinct members $Y_1, \ldots, Y_k$ of the collection, all the 2^k intersections $\bigcap_{j=1}^{k} = Z_j$ are nonempty, where Z_j is either Y_j or $-Y_j$.

For example, a collection C is 2-independent if for every two subsets of C, Y_1 and Y_2, the four sets $Y_1 \cap Y_2$, $-Y_1 \cap Y_2$, $Y_1 \cap -Y_2$, and $-Y_1 \cap -Y_2$ are nonempty. In other words, the fact that a particular element either does or does not belong to a certain set in the collection is not by itself evidence that it does or does not belong to any other set in the collection.

For $A = \{a, b, c, d\}$, the collection $C = \{\{a, b\}, \{a, c\}, \{a, d\}\}$ is a maximal 2-independent collection.

We will now use a result due to Kleitman and Spencer (1973) which states that the size of the maximal k-independent collections is exponential in the number of elements in the set A.

Proposition: *Let (Ω^n, A^n) be a sequence of problems where $|A^n| = n$. For every d, $\beta_d(A^n)$ converges double exponentially to 0 when $n \to \infty$.*

Proof.   By Kleitman and Spencer (1973), there exists a sequence C^n of $(d+1)$-independent collections of subsets of A^n such that the size of C^n is exponential in n. Thus, for every n large enough, the size of C^n is larger than n and, therefore, we can assume that C^n is a cover of A^n (if not, then there exists a set Z in the collection such that any of its members also belongs to another set in the collection; by replacing Z with $A^n - Z$, we obtain a new $(d+1)$-independent collection of subsets of A^n that is a cover of A^n). Let $Q^n = \{q \mid q \in C^n\}$. Since C^n is a cover of A^n, the questionnaire Q^n identifies A^n. No d-implication involving these questions is true in A^n. Thus, $\beta_d(A^n) \leq \alpha_d(Q^n, A^n) = \frac{n}{2^{|Q^n|}}$. $\square$

Note that the proposition refers to any fixed d. If d increases with n, then the result would not necessarily hold (by Claim 3, if $d_n = n - 1$, then $\beta_{d_n}(A^n) \equiv 1$). Note also that there are many sequences of questionnaires that can ensure that the manipulation probability goes to 0. Thus, the principal does not have to choose an optimal questionnaire to make the success of a manipulation very unlikely.

6. Related Literature

The main purpose of this paper is to formally present the intuition that complex questionnaires may assist a principal in eliciting nonverifiable information from agents. In other words, the principal can design a sufficiently complex questionnaire that makes it difficult for dishonest responders to game the system successfully, while treating honest responders fairly.

Kamien and Zemel (1990) is an early paper that models the difficulty of cheating successfully. The most closely related paper to ours is Glazer and Rubinstein (2012). Both that paper and the current one examine a persuasion situation with a boundedly rational agent, although they differ in the procedure used by the agent to come up with a persuasive story. In Glazer and Rubinstein (2012), an agent's profile is a vector of characteristics. The agent is asked to declare a profile after the principal has announced a set of conditions that these characteristics must satisfy for the request to be accepted. The principal's conditions are of the same form as the regularities in the current paper. A crucial assumption in Glazer and Rubinstein (2012) is that the agent's (boundedly rational) procedure of choice is an algorithm that is initiated from his true profile. The principal's problem is to design the set of conditions cleverly enough to be able to differentiate between the agents he wishes to accept and those he wishes to reject. In the current paper, the principal chooses a questionnaire and commits himself to accept a particular set of responses. The agent is limited in his ability to understand the set of acceptable responses. If he decides to lie, he will then fully abandon his true profile and randomly choose a response to the questionnaire that is compatible with the regularities he has detected.

The current paper is related to the growing literature on "behavioral mechanism design." Rubinstein (1993) studies a monopolist's pricing decision where the buyers (modeled using the concept of perceptrons) differ in their ability to process the information contained in a price offer. Glazer and Rubinstein (1998) introduce the idea that the mechanism itself can affect agents' preferences and a designer can sometimes utilize these additional motives to achieve goals he could not otherwise achieve. Eliaz (2002) investigates an implementation problem in which some of the agents are "faulty," in the sense that they fail to act optimally. Piccione and Rubinstein (2003) demonstrate how a discriminatory monopolist can exploit the correlation between a consumer's reservation values and his ability to recognize temporal price patterns. Cabrales and Serrano (2011) look for a mechanism that induces players' actions to converge to the desired outcome when they follow best-response dynamics. Jehiel (2011) shows how an auctioneer, by providing partial information about past bids, can exploit the fact that present bidders see only some of the regularities in the distribution of bids as a function of types. de Clippel (2011) and Korpela (2012) extend standard implementation theory by assuming that agents' decisions are determined by choice functions that are not necessarily rationalizable.

References

Cabrales, A. and R. Serrano (2011): "Implementation in Adaptive Better-Response Dynamics: Towards a General Theory of Bounded Rationality in Mechanisms," *Games and Economic Behavior*, 73, 360–374. [1540]

de Clippel, G. (2011): "Behavioral Implementation," Report. [1541]

Eliaz, K. (2002): "Fault Tolerant Implementation," *Review of Economic Studies,* 69, 589–610. [1540]

Glazer, J. and A. Rubinstein (1998): "Motives and Implementation: On the Design of Mechanisms to Elicit Opinions," *Journal of Economic Theory,* 79, 157–173. [1540]

———— (2012): "A Model of Persuasion With a Boundedly Rational Agent," *Journal of Political Economy,* 120, 1057–1082. [1540]

Jehiel, P. (2011): "Manipulative Auction Design," *Theoretical Economics,* 6, 185–217. [1541]

Kamien, M. I. and E. Zemel (1990): "Tangled Webs: A Note on the Complexity of Compound Lying," Report. [1540]

Kleitman, D. J. and J. Spencer (1973): "Families of k-Independent Sets," *Discrete Mathematics,* 6, 255–262. [1539]

Korpela, V. (2012): "Implementation Without Rationality Assumptions," *Theory and Decision,* 72, 189–203. [1541]

Piccione, M. and A. Rubinstein (2003): "Modeling the Economic Interaction of Agents With Diverse Abilities to Recognize Equilibrium Patterns," *Journal of the European Economic Association,* 1, 212–223. [1540]

Rubinstein, A. (1993): "On Price Recognition and Computational Complexity in a Monopolistic Model," *Journal of Political Economy,* 101, 473–484. [1540]

Printed in the United States
By Bookmasters